New Directions for Adult and Continuing Education

Susan Imel
Jovita M. Ross-Gordon
Coeditors-in-Chief

Adult Education and the Pursuit of Wisdom

D1522267

Elizabeth J. Tisdell
Ann L. Swartz
Editors

Number 131 • Fall 2011
Jossey-Bass
San Francisco

ADULT EDUCATION AND THE PURSUIT OF WISDOM
Elizabeth J. Tisdell, Ann L. Swartz (eds.)
New Directions for Adult and Continuing Education, no. 131
Susan Imel, Jovita M. Ross-Gordon, Coeditors-in-Chief

Microfilm copies of issues and articles are available in 16mm and 35mm, as well as microfiche in 105mm, through University Microfilms Inc., 300 North Zeeb Road, Ann Arbor, Michigan 48106-1346.

NEW DIRECTIONS FOR ADULT AND CONTINUING EDUCATION (ISSN 1052-2891, electronic ISSN 1536-0717) is part of The Jossey-Bass Higher and Adult Education Series and is published quarterly by Wiley Subscription Services, Inc., A Wiley Company, at Jossey-Bass, 989 Market Street, San Francisco, California 94103-1741. Periodicals Postage Paid at San Francisco, California, and at additional mailing offices. POSTMASTER: Send address changes to New Directions for Adult and Continuing Education, Jossey-Bass, 989 Market Street, San Francisco, California 94103-1741.

New Directions for Adult and Continuing Education is indexed in CIJE: Current Index to Journals in Education (ERIC); Contents Pages in Education (T&F); ERIC Database (Education Resources Information Center); Higher Education Abstracts (Claremont Graduate University); and Sociological Abstracts (CSA/CIG).

SUBSCRIPTIONS for print and electronic in the U.S. cost $98.00 for individuals and $316.00 for institutions, agencies, and libraries.

EDITORIAL CORRESPONDENCE should be sent to the Coeditors-in-Chief, Susan Imel, ERIC/ACVE, 1900 Kenny Road, Columbus, Ohio 43210-1090, e-mail: imel.l@osu.edu; or Jovita M. Ross-Gordon, Southwest Texas State University, EAPS Dept., 601 University Drive, San Marcos, TX 78666.

Cover photograph by Jack Hollingsworth@Photodisc

www.josseybass.com

CONTENTS

EDITORS' NOTES

We live in a complex world in need of wisdom. It is a world beset by concerns about unemployment, war and terrorism, environmental and global sustainability, financial instability, and health care reform issues, all of which affect social groups and individuals on physical, emotional, material, and spiritual levels. Adult educators need to work with adult learners, while all of us navigate together in this world ever growing in complexity. How can we do so with wisdom? Wisdom has long been a subject in the world's religious traditions and indigenous cultures, but more recently there has been increased discussion of wisdom in the wider fields of education, neuroscience, psychology, and the humanities. Surprisingly, there has only been a limited consideration of wisdom in the field of adult education. Thus the purpose of this volume is both to consider the nature of wisdom in the different areas relating to adult education by many of the authors who have referred to or discussed wisdom in one way or another in prior work and to consider what such discussions of wisdom might suggest for adult education in various contexts. We have very much enjoyed working with the chapter authors in pondering the nature and mystery of wisdom, and what it might mean for the practice of adult education in the complexity of changing times.

As coeditors of the volume, in the first two chapters, we attempt to theoretically ground the discussion. In the first chapter, Elizabeth Tisdell provides an overview of the literature on the nature of wisdom, and juxtaposes it with the wisdom of nature. She then offers her perceptions on some current issues in the field of adult education and considers what an understanding of wisdom that embraces paradox and complexity might offer for living our way into the further development of adult education.

In Chapter Two, Ann Swartz looks to neuroscience and an evolutionary perspective on sacred knowing to explore the connection between embodied learning and wisdom. The chapter examines ways in which the understandings gleaned from current brain imaging studies intersect with both Eastern and Western traditions for attaining wisdom. It then explores the emotion of wonder as an element present in the wisdom traditions of the major religions, as well as indigenous and nature religions, raising questions about the wisest ways to survive today while keeping our evolved "social brain" intact.

Chapters Three and Four, respectively, deal with transcendent and practical wisdom. Wilma Fraser and Tara Hyland-Russell, in Chapter Three, focus on the figure of Sophia, often associated with transcendent wisdom, and invoke her as metaphorical guide. They describe a path for educators and practitioners that can assist in the recovery of wisdom in the face of increasing pressures of statistical and other measurable outcomes within the field of lifelong learning. They also invite a more personal rediscovery of the ancient persona, Sophia. In Chapter Four, Caroline Bassett, the Director of the Wisdom Institute, begins by offering an overview of research on wisdom and strategies that educators can employ to foster the development of wisdom in themselves and in their students. She presents the view that it is practical wisdom that helps us get through difficult situations in ways that enhance our common humanity.

Chapters Five and Six draw on Eastern, Western, and Mideastern cultural and religious perspectives to develop a fuller understanding of wisdom. In Chapter Five, Shih-ying Yang draws on her research on wisdom in both the United States and Taiwan and her experience and knowledge of cognitive psychology and wisdom. She discusses Eastern and Western perspectives on wisdom as a process necessary to strive for a "good life," and then explores what it means to educate adults in cross-cultural settings. In Chapter Six, Abraham Sussman and Mitchell Kossak discuss the psychology of the inner life, and how music, dance, sacred chant, and meditation from different religious and cultural traditions can tap into unitive states of being that lead to inner wisdom. Illustrating with personal and case examples from clinical practice, they introduce transpersonal psychology to the discussion.

Chapters Seven and Eight take on aspects of gender and/or culture in relation to wisdom, though they do so in quite different ways. In Chapter Seven, Chinwe Okpalaoka and Cynthia Dillard explore how the spiritual and cultural contexts of wisdom and Black women's knowing can facilitate both cross-cultural and within-group understandings of race, gender, and identity in teaching and learning. They do so by setting up their chapter as a dialogue about race and their experience of unfolding wisdom in a classroom context in which they were both involved that drew on multiple ways of knowing. In Chapter Eight, Laurent Parks Daloz begins his consideration of mentoring men toward wisdom, with his own experience of being mentored by an older male. He then argues that mentoring men toward wisdom entails transformation of the pillars of traditional masculinity—procreating, providing, and protecting—and considers what such a transformation might mean for working with men as adult learners.

In the closing chapter, well-known author on issues in adult education and lifelong education Peter Jarvis pulls the volume together, providing reflections on the human quest to understand both the "why" and the "how" of existence itself as the pull toward wisdom; however, he cautions that while we can be taught about wisdom, we can only learn to be wise by embracing the experience of life itself. As coeditors of this volume, we heartily agree! But we believe that by pondering the nature and mystery of wisdom, and its integrative, paradoxical, and multidisciplinary quality, that we can perhaps live our way into wiser thinking and living, as we continue to forge the field of adult education.

Acknowledgments

We'd like to thank all the authors for their insights, hard work, and wise counsel in putting together this volume on wisdom. In addition, we'd especially like to thank graduate assistants Irma Hunt and Debrah Krauss for editing and proofreading each of these chapters.

Elizabeth J. Tisdell
Ann L. Swartz
Editors

ELIZABETH J. TISDELL is a professor of adult education and the coordinator of the Adult Education Doctoral Program at Penn State University–Harrisburg.

ANN L. SWARTZ is an instructor of nursing and an affiliate assistant professor of adult education at Penn State University–Harrisburg.

1

This chapter introduces the volume and provides an overview of the literature on the nature of wisdom and the wisdom of nature as weaving webs of connection and embracing paradox that can offer insight to current trends in adult education.

The Wisdom of Webs A-Weaving: Adult Education and the Paradoxes of Complexity in Changing Times

Elizabeth J. Tisdell

Nature seems to have its own wisdom. The world turns, the sun rises and sets every day, and seasons change in reliable mystery as life unfolds in a series of spiraling cycles. Most of the time we pay no attention to these earthly rhythms and are just caught up in the tasks of daily life. But occasionally, something catches us off guard, like the mysterious weavings of a yellow garden spider, and we find ourselves agog contemplating the wonder of nature and what such "nature wisdom" might teach us for daily living, or even for our work with adult learners.

A couple of years ago, upon returning home from a summer away to begin again one of those similar but not so mysterious cycles—that of academic life—I unlocked my back door, only to observe the glorious webbed handiwork of one of these garden spider beauties connecting the branches of the rosebush outside my sunroom window. In the middle, there she was, huge and yellow, guarding the web of her own home and the sunroom window of mine. At first, I was afraid of her in all her big-fuzziness; but then learned she was harmless to humans and very beneficial to gardens. She became "Charlotte," and over the next couple of weeks, Charlotte and her handiwork, which glistened like stained glass in the summer sun, became part of my daily observation. If anything came near or touched her web, she would oscillate the entire lattice, sometimes catching something for dinner. Any damage and Charlotte would busily make repairs; she'd respin, reweave, and reconnect. And so it went over the next several days—until alas—one day at summer's end, Charlotte was nowhere to be found. Likely

New Directions for Adult and Continuing Education, no. 131, Fall 2011 © 2011 Wiley Periodicals, Inc.
Published online in Wiley Online Library (wileyonlinelibrary.com) • DOI: 10.1002/ace.416

she had laid her eggs and died, as the very next year, when I returned for a new cycle of academic life, there was another yellow garden spider in the middle of a finely spun orb outside my sunroom window—perhaps Charlotte's daughter! And so began a new cycle of study, not only of the spinning and spawning of yellow garden spiders, but of the *cyclic webs of nature* that offer both scientific and metaphorical explanations about the interconnection of all things. Such was one of many lessons in lifelong learning, all through the web weaving of yellow garden spiders!

What has this to do with adult education and with wisdom? Wisdom indeed is difficult to define. It is associated with age and experience (Erikson and Erikson, 1997), yet it is not limited to either of these. There is also an integrative quality to wisdom, a sense of weaving together many (sometimes disparate) threads into a new coherent whole. Hall (2010) highlights the paradoxical dimension of wisdom and observes: "It is rooted in character, personal history, and the experience of human nature, yet it is bigger than any one individual. It exists as both edifice and fog, is both immortal yet fleeting . . ." (p. 23). Such is the elusive *nature of wisdom*. But there is also the *wisdom of nature* that we so often miss. Yet it is ever present in its ability to rejuvenate itself, for as complexity scientist Frijtof Capra (1996) notes, living systems—whether individual cells, entire human bodies, or fields of study—survive by creating new patterns of connection: They repair, reorganize, and reweave new connecting threads in the web of life, just as garden spiders do as part of their innate wisdom. Thus, the *wisdom of nature* might offer us some insight into the paradoxical and ever elusive *nature of wisdom*.

Surprisingly, there has been only limited consideration of wisdom in the field of adult education (Jarvis, 2001; Barrett, 2005), though Merriam Caffaralla, and Baumgartner (2007) synthesized some of it in relation to adult development drawing from cognitive psychology. There is a developing discussion of wisdom, however, in the wider education discourses (Sternberg and Jordan, 2005). In this era of globalization and academic downsizing, it is perhaps useful to consider what it might mean to educate adults for wisdom and to attend to it in our daily lives as lifelong learners. Adult education is an interdisciplinary field; it is ripe for weaving new patterns of connection not only among ourselves but also with numerous fields of study, from science to religion and beyond. I am hoping that we can do so with wisdom. As daunting as it is to edit a volume on wisdom and adult education, I'll begin by providing an overview of the literature on wisdom itself and then consider what some of its insights might suggest for dealing with a few current challenges facing the field of adult education; some chapter authors do so with greater specificity. This chapter is grounded in two basic assumptions: that there is an integration quality to wisdom that attends to the hidden wholeness and interconnectedness of everything in the universe; and that wisdom is based on the type of knowledge that makes these web-like connections more visible in creative ways.

New Directions for Adult and Continuing Education • DOI: 10.1002/ace

The Nature of Wisdom: An Overview

There is a body of literature that tries to attempt to define the ever-elusive nature of wisdom, much of it referring to insights from many of the world's great religions and indigenous cultures (Smith, 1991; Schussler Fiorenza, 2001); indeed, questions of how to live in a way that makes life meaningful have been with us since humans appeared on Earth and are thus the subject of most of the world's religions. There are also numerous references to wisdom in the professional literature in medicine, management, and education that focus on how practitioners can apply practical knowledge in artful ways (Sternberg, 2003; Bassett, 2005). Several authors in this volume discuss the overall literature and research outlining the nature of wisdom; here, as I have also done elsewhere (Tisdell, 2011), I summarize the main themes.

Forms of Wisdom: The Transcendent and the Practical. Wisdom as it connects to knowledge has been the subject of both philosophy and religion; indeed, the very root of the word "philosophy" means "love of wisdom." Often cited in discussions are the Aristotelian distinctions among its types—primarily between *Sophia*, as transcendent wisdom, and *phronesis*, as practical wisdom; occasionally, *episteme*, as theoretical or scientific wisdom, is mentioned as well (Osbeck and Robinson, 2005). A common reference in discussions of *Sophia* (as spiritual or transcendent wisdom) is from Proverbs 24 of the Hebrew Bible, where Wisdom is building *her* house and carving out seven pillars.

Authors who discuss wisdom also often recount the story of Socrates, who was seen by his contemporaries as having knowledge and wisdom but who denied being knowledgeable or wise. Hence, humility is deemed a characteristic of wisdom. This tension of wisdom as having knowledge, but recognizing that at the same time one does not have knowledge, since all knowledge is partial, connects wisdom (in the *Sophia* sense) to the notion of paradox. Goldberg (2005) discusses the "paradox of wisdom" (the paradox being that the "older" brain becomes more wise) from a neuroscience perspective (discussed further by Swartz, this volume), arguing that adults who age well make decisions based more on pattern recognition as a result of the complex neural patterns that develop over time. Such patterns allow for drawing on multiple parts of the brain at the same time, resulting in wiser ways of being in the world. In essence, Goldberg examines wisdom from a scientific perspective. Others look at wisdom as integration; Palmer (2004), for example, encourages people to pay attention to the hidden wholeness within. Many authors also discuss how to cultivate wisdom, either in the *phronesis* sense of practical wisdom (discussed further by Bassett, this volume) or in the *Sophia* sense of the metaphysical which has implications for adult education (discussed by Fraser and Hyland-Russell, this volume). But across all of these discussions, there is an integration quality to wisdom that allows people to negotiate opposites in creative ways that lead to more integrative thinking and an ability to deal with paradox.

These notions of wisdom—*Sophia* as transcendental or the highest form of knowledge and *phronesis* as practical knowledge—cannot be separated, as one often leads to the other, as part of the interconnecting web of wisdom of the universe itself. As Yang (this volume) notes, the wisdom embraced by a culture or religion (in its most positive sense) offers insights for practically how to live a "good life." In his recent memoir, world religions scholar Huston Smith (2010) highlights what he learned not only from scholarly work, but also from embracing practices from the world's religions to *experience* their wisdom. He highlights how they related to his ability to access wonder—from the chants of Hinduism, to Buddhist meditations on the present moment, to the dances of the Sufis, the mysteries of the Tao, and on meditations out of the Judeo-Christian Biblical tradition. As he notes, "Most mystics don't want to *read* religious wisdom: they want to *be it*. A postcard of a beautiful lake is not a beautiful lake," and then explains: "What drew me to the Sufis was in fact their dancing, how they pray not merely with their minds but with their bodies" (p. 147). Indeed, wisdom is not simply of the mind; it is also embodied in music, dance, and meditation (discussed further by Sussman and Kossak, this volume). Interestingly, as many neuroscientists have recently noted (e.g., Siegel, 2010), meditation and embodied practices change the structure of the brain as it weaves new neural patterns of connection, just as spiders do as they reweave their webs.

To be clear, Smith is in no way suggesting that embracing meditation and other embodied practices as a way of accessing wisdom means completely suspending the rational mind; indeed, critical thinking and having content knowledge as competence to act in the world is part of the way of practical wisdom, and exercising judgment. As many scholars note, embodied spiritual practices, along with rational critical thought, should inspire people and lead to wise action to promote equity and justice in the world (Schussler Fiorenza, 2001), a point Okpalaoka and Dillard (this volume) also discuss. But human beings are not likely to be inspired by academic knowledge alone, which is distinct from wisdom. As Patricia Hill Collins (1990) points out, "In the context of race, gender, and class oppression, the distinction is essential. Knowledge without wisdom is adequate for the powerful, but wisdom is essential to the survival of the subordinate" (p. 208). The point then is to embrace the paradox of both action and nonaction (stillness in the present moment), both rationality and nonrationality, and to be opened to greater wisdom as a result for action in the world.

Wisdom, Education, and Adult Development. There is a growing discussion in recent years about *educating* for wisdom and attending to how it develops. Sternberg and Jordan (2005) in their edited collection focus on wisdom largely from a cognitive psychology perspective (more in the *phronesis* than the *Sophia* sense) in regard to cross-cultural theories of wisdom, its development across the lifespan, and its presence in practice in workplaces.

Contributors to Ferrari and Potworowski's (2008) anthology focus more specifically on cross-cultural perspectives on *teaching* for wisdom.

In many publications and edited collections (Young-Eisendrath and Miller, 2000; Mijares, 2003), authors consider wisdom from a developmental psychology perspective drawing on the work of Erik Erikson (who saw wisdom as a desired end state of development) and discuss it in relation to maturity and/or spirituality. In a similar vein, drawing on her husband's work as well as her own as an artist, Joan Erikson (1991) weaves together the connection among wisdom, creativity, and sensory experience. She highlights several qualities of wisdom, including interdependence, resilience, empathy, humor, and humility, as well as artistic practices that help facilitate identity development and wisdom as well as help negotiate the paradoxes of living. In particular, she contemplates the paradox of the wise fool, and what it means to embrace dialectics to deal with life's limitations. Being pulled open beyond the limitations of such polarities as rational/affective, action/stillness, male/female by embracing both sides of the dialectic is a hallmark of wisdom, she argues, and has implications for how we continue to live in the world. Daloz (this volume) explores what this might mean for mentoring men's ongoing development toward wisdom.

There have been several research studies on wisdom, how it develops, and what it suggests for wise practice. The contributors to this volume summarize these and offer insights on what wisdom means for them in various adult education venues, while Jarvis, in the closing chapter, discusses what it suggests for further directions in lifelong learning, though he notes the distinction between learning *about* wisdom and being wise. In the remainder of this chapter, I offer some thoughts on what the literature on wisdom might suggest in light of some current issues in the field.

Adult Education and Wisdom

In thinking about wisdom in relation to the field of adult education, it is helpful to consider its current academic landscape in order to begin to vision the future, hopefully with greater wisdom. While I've discussed much of this elsewhere (see Tisdell, 2011), I do so here in greater detail.

Recent Trends and Current Issues. Like any field of study, recent publications tell us something about its current emphases. In the past 10 years there has been much discussion on different theoretical perspectives on adult education, such as on how one's social location affects teaching and learning from various critical, feminist, race-centered, postmodern, or other sociocultural perspectives. This has resulted in numerous journal publications, as well as the new *Handbook of Race and Adult Education* (edited by Sheared, Johnson-Bailey, Colin, Peterson, and Brookfield, 2010), which gives an in-depth look at issues of race and ethnicity. Merriam and Grace (2011) have put together a collection on contemporary issues in the field, and of course the recent *Handbook of Adult and Continuing Education* (Kasworm, Rose, and Ross-Gordon, 2010) that focuses on the centrality of adult learning in various contexts of practice tell us something of important current issues in the field. Further, the increasing attention to how factors such as emotions, spirituality, the arts, popular culture, and the body relate to adult development and learning offer new insight about how to teach and learn more holistically, which can relate to the interconnecting web that may lead to educating with greater wisdom.

Recent publications do tell us something of the current issues in the field; yet it is more often at conferences that one gets more of a *feeling* for what is really hot for the people in a field—what people's passions and concerns are. The flash in their eyes or excitement in their voices when presenting their scholarship is a much greater indicator of what generates life for them than can ever come alive in the flatness of a printed page. People's frustrations also become apparent, sometimes coming out in sarcastic remarks or in rolling eyes at general sessions, or in less formal conversations among close colleagues. In my own experience in these gatherings at conferences over the past 20 years (which indicates that I have experience, but not necessarily wisdom!) it is clear there are many positive things happening. But there are a few challenges or tendencies of concern that I have observed or heard articulated, likely reflective of larger issues in academia (also discussed elsewhere, Tisdell, 2011), namely: about the decline of academic adult education positions; that academia is big on critique of positions, and sometimes shorter on solution and inspiration; that there tends to be an emphasis on difference and division than on what integrates or unites. How might we deal with some of these issues with greater wisdom?

Embracing Paradox, the Nature of Wisdom, and the Wisdom of Nature. The literature outlining the nature of wisdom suggests that part of the solution might lie in the notion of paradox: that embracing the tension of the opposite and engaging the dialectic perhaps pulls us open to greater creativity and wisdom. Indeed, many of the authors cited here have referred to the apparent paradoxes of wisdom, such as: The more that one knows, one realizes the limits of one's knowledge; within scarcity, there is abundance; to lose oneself is to find oneself. Paradoxically, losing our identity as a field may also be a way to find it anew; this fits well with the notion of emergence that arises out of complexity science.

Most of the literature outlining the *nature of wisdom* ignores the *wisdom of nature*. But complexity scientists emphasize the patterns of connection within nature and the ways that living systems self-organize to adapt and survive; they marvel at the wonder and *wisdom of nature* in some of its aspects, of the mystery of the swarm of ants or locusts (Fisher, 2009; Mitchell, 2009)—of the limited intelligence of a single ant but of the "super intelligence" of huge ant colonies that constantly reorganize to ensure their survival. Perhaps this is instinct, not wisdom. But contemplation of these patterns of nature can lead to its own wisdom. Further, complexity scientists suggest that these emergent and new patterns of connection offer insights for human reorganization, which may have implications for adult education in changing times.

There are certainly concerns about funding, the closing of graduate degree programs in adult education, and the lack of replacement for faculty who retire or leave an institution, or the "reorganization" of adult education via absorption into other departments. But if the old adage that a crisis is both a danger and an opportunity is true, it might behoove us to think about the "opportunities" before us in these times of scarce resources and "reorganization," and to consider some of the thinking from complexity science (Capra, 1996)—that living systems self-organize to create new patterns of connection. While one can indeed be marginalized at the beginning in reorganized departments, there are also great opportunities for collaboration. The more we collaborate with others in professional fields, such as medicine, health care, or business (disciplines in which there is more emphasis on curricular content than on pedagogy), the more we have the opportunity to really influence the education of adults in multiple disciplines and settings. There is also typically more grant funding available in such content-driven fields, and collaborating with colleagues can lead to further creative thinking and webs of connection.

Secondly, the fact that we are a field that encourages critique of positions is indeed a strength; it is important to rationally consider the strengths and weaknesses of a particular position and make apparent its theoretical underpinnings or assumptions. Nevertheless, too often critique as it is practiced tears apart a particular position highlighting only what is wrong with it. While sharp and focused critical thinking grounded in rationality is absolutely necessary, and requires analysis of the parts, rationality alone is not a substitute for wisdom, nor will it inspire people toward hope that sustains efforts toward the creation of something new, as the research on transformative learning tells us. Rather, change and creativity are borne of experience of the *whole* and the integration of the parts in new-woven patterns of connection. It doesn't come *only* from rational critique. It also comes from weaving new and more complex patterns of neuro-firing among various parts of the learning brain to express what generates life and creativity such as the way art, music, dance, or poetic expression does. Thus, I believe we also need to focus on what is good about a position as well as what is weak about it, and to provide examples of inspiration in the very positions we critique. This can happen not only through logical academic presentation, but also through creative expression. This is part of living the dialectic; it does not mean giving up rational critique. It is simply part of embracing the tension of opposites. Thus, perhaps wisdom might suggest adopting a new mantra: "Critique, but create!"

The third concern, that we tend to focus more on what separates than what integrates, is probably borne of the other two: particularly the emphasis on rational critique that requires separating out positions into parts or categories. We often focus on what separates us from other related fields (such as human resource development), or what separates us into groups of people by culture, gender, or race. It is extremely important to examine the differences in underlying theoretical perspectives among different and related disciplines and to do research on the needs of specific groups of learners based on social location. Indeed, we are not simply generic people with exactly the same learning needs. Nevertheless, there tends to be a lack of consideration of what is also common among us, across disciplines or social location. This is perhaps where we can take a cue from complexity science. As Capra (1996) suggests in his discussion of the web of life, surviving, adapting, and thriving in the great web of life is borne of weaving new webs of connection to create a unique whole. It is what allows an organism to thrive, perhaps all part of being mindful of the hidden wholeness within.

Conclusion

In conclusion, there is literature both on the nature of wisdom and the wisdom of nature. But literature only tells us what something is *about*; wisdom comes about from wise *living* through embracing tensions of opposites, as well as wonder, mystery, and complexity. Wisdom involves both head knowledge and soul knowledge; it is what helps us weave together connections within our own being, and in human relations with others as individuals and across gender, culture, race, and religious differences and academic disciplines to facilitate wise action. It is about embracing paradox and dialectics that potentially pulls us open to something new—and to our very creativity. It is not borne of rationality *alone*, nor of meditation *alone* (or other practices of creative expression that get us into an altered state of consciousness). Rather, it is borne of an integration of these multiple ways of knowing, which allows us to both critique and create as we engage (hopefully) in wise action in the world. I have great hopes for the field of adult education as we forge together our future by embracing paradox with its both/and thinking. May we draw on the wisdom of *Sophia*, the critique and practical know-how or *phronesis* that our field is known for, as well as the humility of Socrates! We can take our cue, not only by reflecting on the nature of wisdom, but also by observing the wisdom of nature. Indeed, perhaps we'll discover new ways to both critique and create, with mystery, passion, and wonder along the way—not only at yellow garden spiders weaving their mysterious webs, but at the ways that adult educators are also weaving new webs of connections leading to further emergence. The chapter authors in this volume tell us something of how they are thinking about wisdom. Hopefully, it will spawn ways to further weave the web of adult education in a unique pattern that emerges in greater wisdom.

New Directions for Adult and Continuing Education • DOI: 10.1002/ace

References

Bassett, C. "Emergent Wisdom: Living a Life in Widening Circles." *ReVision*, 2005, 27(4), 3–11.

Capra, F. *The Web of Life: A New Scientific Understanding of Living Systems.* New York: Random House, 1996.

Collins, P. H. *Black Feminist Thought.* New York: Routledge, 1990.

Erikson, E., and Erikson, J. *The Lifecycle Completed.* New York: W.W. Norton & Company, 1997.

Erikson, J. *Wisdom and the Senses.* New York: W.W. Norton & Company, 1991.

Ferrari, M., & Potworowski, G. (eds.). *Teaching for Wisdom: Cross-Cultural Perspectives on Fostering Wisdom.* New York: Springer, 2008.

Fisher, L. *The Perfect Swarm: The Science of Complexity in Everyday Life.* New York: Basic Books, 2009.

Goldberg, E. *The Wisdom Paradox.* New York: Gotham Books, 2005.

Hall, S. *Wisdom: From Philosophy to Neuroscience.* New York: Knopf, 2010.

Jarvis, P. *Learning in Later Life.* London: Kogan Paul, 2001.

Kasworm, C., Rose, A., and Ross-Gordon, J. (eds.). *Handbook of Adult and Continuing Education*, 2010 edition. Thousand Oaks, Calif.: Sage, 2010.

Merriam, S., Caffarella, R., and Baumgartner, L. *Learning in Adulthood: A Comprehensive Guide.*, (3rd ed.) San Francisco: Jossey-Bass, 2007.

Merriam, S., and Grace, A. (ed.). *The Jossey-Bass Reader on Contemporary Issues in Adult Education.* San Francisco: Jossey-Bass, 2011.

Mijares, S. (ed.). *Modern Psychology and Ancient Wisdom.* Binghamton, N.Y.: Haworth Press, Inc., 2003.

Mitchell, M. *Complexity: A Guided Tour.* New York: Oxford University Press, 2009.

Osbeck, L. M., and Robinson, D. "Philosophical Theories of Wisdom." In R. Sternberg and J. Jordan (eds.), *A Handbook of Wisdom* (pp. 61–83). New York: Cambridge University Press, 2005.

Palmer, P. *A Hidden Wholeness.* San Francisco: Jossey-Bass, 2004.

Schussler Fiorenza, E. *Wisdom Ways: Feminist Biblical Interpretation.* Maryknoll, N.Y.: Orbis, 2001.

Sheared, V., Johnson-Bailey, J., Colin, S., Peterson, E., and Brookfield, S. (eds.). *The Handbook of Race and Adult Education.* San Francisco: Jossey-Bass, 2010.

Siegel, D. *Mindsight: The New Science of Personal Transformation.* New York: Random House, 2010.

Smith, H. *The World's Religions: Our Great Wisdom Traditions.* San Francisco: Harper-Collins, 1991.

Smith, H. *Tales of Wonder.* San Francisco: HarperCollins, 2010.

Sternberg, R. *Wisdom, Intelligence, and Creativity Synthesized.* New York: Cambridge University Press, 2003.

Sternberg, R., and Jordan, J. (eds.). *A Handbook of Wisdom.* New York: Cambridge University Press, 2005.

Tisdell, E. "Working Toward Wisdom in Changing Times: Embracing Paradox and Possibility in the Field of Adult Education." In A. Mandell (ed.), *Occasional Papers: Exploration in Adult Higher Education.* Saratoga Springs, N.Y.: SUNY Empire State College, 2011.

Young-Eisendrath, P., and Miller, M. (eds.). *The Psychology of Mature Spirituality: Integrity, Wisdom, Transcendence.* New York: Routledge, 2000.

ELIZABETH J. TISDELL *is a professor of adult education and the coordinator of the Adult Education Doctoral Program at Penn State University–Harrisburg.*

2

This chapter looks to neuroscience and an evolutionary perspective on sacred knowing to explore the connection between embodied learning and wisdom.

Wisdom, the Body, and Adult Learning: Insights from Neuroscience

Ann L. Swartz

Years ago, as I struggled along to adapt after a head injury, I marveled at the gap between my interior experience and outward presentation. Two decades later, I found myself following my body's guidance to move, breathe, reflect, and be outdoors, to heal my mind, which was disconnected by sleep deprivation and stress. These life experiences showed me that my body possessed wisdom. Recently, facing breast cancer that my body identified when technology failed to do so, I was awestruck by more manifestations of wisdom. My exhausted body managed to tell me what to eat. My fears were calmed by unique spiritual experiences of connection that reassured me that I was not going to die, not yet, not from this. The outpouring of empathy from so many people was expressed in caring behavior but also was evident in the openness of my wise caring others' eyes—a look I associated with childhood because of its openness, less frequently seen in adults. It was the look of compassion, an action component of wisdom. Cognizance of the evolution of my own bodily wisdom made it simple to embrace the evolutionary understanding of embodied wisdom that appears in science. This science is the story I will try to share in this chapter, along with its connection to wisdom and embodied learning. This is not a personal story, but rather a portion of the science that helped me understand, accept, and adapt to my changing body experience.

In adult education, there has recently been a recognition of the body's role in adult learning (Merriam, Caffarella, and Baumgartner, 2007). Attention to neuroscience is somewhat limited, though is emerging (Johnson and Taylor, 2006). These two perspectives are not integrated. With this chapter, I will argue that adult education must look to science to achieve a deeper understanding of the evolving neurobiological body and its connection to

New Directions for Adult and Continuing Education, no. 131, Fall 2011 © 2011 Wiley Periodicals, Inc.
Published online in Wiley Online Library (wileyonlinelibrary.com) • DOI: 10.1002/ace.417

wisdom. The chapter will weave together threads of embodied learning, wisdom, and neuroscience, all grounded in the assumption that wisdom arises from the body. The chapter begins with historical context, indentifies a neuroscience definition of wisdom, summarizes neurobiological development of wisdom, and presents examples of embodied practice linked to transcendent wisdom and neuroscience.

Historical Context

Long before humankind embarked on its remarkable efforts to codify our understanding of the world and provide a basis for scholarly reflection and debate, our ancestors knew the world through bodily prehension. They recognized that which is greater than all of us by prehending a whole universe. They experienced themselves as embedded in the natural world by way of what cultural historian Morris Berman (2000) labels "paradoxical" consciousness (p. 9). Paradoxical consciousness is an experience of space, a diffuse peripheral awareness that accepts the world as it presents itself, implying trust. It is a way of being simultaneously focused and nonfocused that allows a sense of connection with the natural world, a perception described elsewhere in connection with wonder (Taylor, 2007). Wonder may be a manifestation of wisdom. The diffuse awareness of paradoxical consciousness is consistent with preconscious, unlanguaged embodied knowing as described by embodied cognitive science (Varela, Thompson, and Rosch, 1991).

Genetic anthropology (Behar, 2008) shows that our early human ancestors share a limited gene pool and a common African mother. Lineages outside Africa descended from a very small band who left that place maybe 70,000 years ago (Behar, 2008), when the artifact record suggests that paradoxical consciousness was probably still in place (Berman, 2000). Berman (2000) proposes that when paradoxical consciousness was the norm, the Sacred existed within the natural world. Later generations understood the Sacred as being above and outside their world and sought reconnection through religious and mystical experiences (Berman, 2000).

In recent writing about conscious mind, neuroscientist Antonio Damasio (2010) also takes an evolutionary perspective, writing that over millions of years of nervous system evolution, people eventually developed awareness of themselves as separate from their environment and each other. Increasing population size created selective pressure for nervous system features promoting social connection. These social connection survival skills formed the neural basis of our current human brain, the social brain (Damasio, 2010). Wisdom is now a label given to the social brain's capabilities (Meeks and Jeste, 2009).

Neuroscience Defining Wisdom

Neuroscience is new to the study of wisdom. Definitions of wisdom vary, and scientific research requires a specific operational definition. Meeks and

Jeste (2009), two physician researchers, created one by reviewing empirical studies of wisdom from several disciplines. From these studies, they identified the components of wisdom. Then they selected studies that used brain imaging, examined neurotransmitters, or considered genetics. These studies sourced their definition.

Meeks and Jeste (2009) operationally define wisdom as a unique psychological trait comprised of subcomponents, all adaptive human attributes. They identify characteristics consistent with psychology research (Hall, 2010), and list these components: prosocial attitudes and behaviors of empathy, compassion, altruism; rational decision making based on pragmatic knowledge of life; emotional stability; insight/self-reflection; tolerance of divergent value systems; decisiveness when facing uncertainty (Meeks and Jeste, 2009; Jeste and Harris, 2010). The term *prosocial behaviors* emphasizes the psychology findings, as discussed in Hall (2010), that wisdom is selfless action, not just having feelings of empathy, compassion, or altruism.

This is arguably a working definition of practical wisdom that leaves epistemic and transcendent wisdom untouched. Others might see the attention to social behavior and experience as an overlap with transcendent wisdom. Meeks and Jeste (2009) acknowledge this limitation. They selected only the most frequently occurring concepts, eliminating epistemology, religiosity, and intuition. Theirs is, of necessity, a definition derived from published research and is expected to change over time with the accumulation of new evidence. Jeste's collaborator, Harris (2009), has made an opening to address transcendent wisdom with neuroscience. He describes transcendent wisdom as the possible outcome of following a prescribed spiritual path that facilitates emotional maturity. He identifies an experience component to this wisdom, sought by following a path: a heightened sense of inner silence, joy, gratitude, and spontaneous morality. Harris (2009) connects this wisdom to Eastern and Western religions that teach constraint, disciplined morality, charitable concern, and compassionate action.

Harkening back to William James's 1905 lectures on the "Varieties of Religious Experience" as the first example linking neurology and religion, Harris (2009) begins to pave the way for connecting transcendent wisdom to the subjective sense of self, meditative practice, and a search to experience the hidden wholeness. This is all theoretical background thinking, but within a neuroscience group that finds wisdom interesting (Meeks & Jeste, 2009; Jeste & Harris, 2010). In light of Harris (2009) linking transcendent wisdom to experience while on a spiritual path, it is of note that Giordano and Engebretson (2006) completed a review of research similar to the one by Meeks and Jeste (2009) to identify neural and cognitive correlates of spiritual experience. They uncovered diverse, culturally embedded forms of intentionally altered states of consciousness that shared a common, specific neural pathway. As with the practical wisdom Meeks and Jeste (2009) described, the prefrontal cortex is involved. But these spiritual experiences also activated the temporal and parietal areas. This very different brain event may or may not be an aspect of transcendental wisdom, but does beg for more research.

Wisdom is further understood, neurobiologically, as an emergent property of integrated brain functioning (Cozolino, 2006; Jeste and Harris, 2010). This means that knowing the components, the associated brain areas and chemicals, and genetics is not enough to understand wisdom. Wisdom arises spontaneously from these parts in interaction, and how this happens is a mystery, just as emergence of mind and consciousness remain mysteries to science (Damasio, 2010). Meeks and Jeste (2009) also write that wisdom exists in the population on a continuum, but don't offer details. This might seem to contradict the cultural construction of the paradoxical "wise fool" as he appears in Shakespeare's plays, but it could also reflect the relative specificity and rigidity of scientific definition versus social labeling. Only somewhat stable in each individual, the wisdom trait is primarily shaped by experience and learning, the same being true for the brain's cortex (Meeks and Jeste, 2009). This complexity makes wisdom a very difficult construct to unravel.

By integrating the neuroscience research on components of wisdom, Meeks and Jeste (2009) produced a model to ground future research. Their model emphasizes brain function, reflecting the empirical literature but with the understanding that the nervous system flows throughout the body, and embodied mind arises from its integrated functioning. This neurobiological model identifies two brain regions commonly activated to produce the subcomponents of wisdom: the prefrontal cortex, the most recently evolved part of the brain; and the limbic striatum, a most ancient brain area, associated with fear regulation. These two areas must connect with neural circuits and balance each other's activities to create subjective awareness and emotional self-regulation, precursors to wisdom. The anterior cingulate is also involved in conflict identification, emotional stability, and wise decision making.

Development of neural connections among these areas requires experiences. We need a wealth of experiences to become wise. Damage to these connections and their regulatory systems are often found in traumatic stress disorders (Siegel, 2010), so trauma can interfere with wisdom. Neurochemicals related to mental health—dopamine and serotonin—are also critical to constructing the components of wisdom. Neurochemical activity is strongly influenced by genetic factors. Meeks and Jeste (2009) document that impulsivity is 45 percent heritable and that prosocial behaviors, such as altruism, are 50 to 60 percent heritable. We might look to our parents and grandparents to understand our own resources for wisdom.

Developing Wisdom

Understanding wisdom's lifetime developmental trajectory from a neuroscience perspective requires looking more deeply into prefrontal cortex function and its mirror neurons. Jacobani (2008) describes his research on these specialized neurons that help to connect what we see with what we feel through touch. When we see someone toss a ball, the neural activity in our brains is the same as if we tossed the ball ourselves. Mirror neurons seem to be related to wisdom because they help us empathize (Meeks and Jeste, 2009). This automatic mirroring is the basis of our learning by observing, as well as of our ability to put ourselves in another's place and sometimes even to feel their pain.

Interpersonal neurobiology adherents like Cozolino (2006) and Siegel (2010) also attend to mirror neurons because they make resonance behaviors possible. These psychiatric practitioner-researchers describe how mirror neurons help us echo each other's movements, facial expressions, and sounds in ways that attune us to each other. Mirror neurons allow us to behave wisely and to express prosocial attitudes and behavior like empathy. Mirror neurons are critical to the early life-nurturing relationships that shape the wisdom-capable brain (Cozolino, 2006). They also give us access to inner body awareness and intuition, abilities that help us make wise connections with other people and with ourselves (Siegel, 2010).

Many cultures view older people as wiser, but reviews of empirical literature find inconclusive results (Hall, 2010; Jeste and Harris, 2010). Are we, in some ways, born wise? Two different perspectives indicate that we are born with the gift of the neurobiological seeds of wisdom. First, in their seminal book about embodied cognition, Varela, Thompson, and Rosch (1991) point out that in the evolutionary past, West and East shared a common Indo-European heritage in which philosophy was not abstract but was tied to disciplined methods for knowing, including mindfulness as a natural state of awareness. They explain that when experiencing mindfulness, mind is present in embodied everyday experience, not preoccupied with theorizing or worrying. The basic nature of the mind is assumed to be mindful awareness. We can learn habitual patterns that distract us, but disciplines such as meditation return the mind to its natural characteristic of knowing itself and reflecting its experience. "This is the beginning of *prajna,* the Sanskrit word for wisdom in both Hindu and Buddhist traditions" (Varela, Thompson, and Rosch, 1991, p. 26). It is interesting to note that this description of mindful awareness has similarities to Berman's (2000) paradoxical consciousness; both are grounded in an evolutionary understanding of human mind. This suggests a possible connection between wisdom and the concept of paradoxical consciousness that could be explored.

A second and harmonizing perspective comes from interpersonal neurobiology (Cozolino, 2006; Siegel, 2010) that assumes the brain is an evolved social organ. Brain plasticity, the ability of the brain to change itself subject to experience, and mechanisms of survival are key. Plasticity provides for the social construction of the brain, especially within attachment relationships. Cozolino (2006) writes that human survival equals nurturance, since early nurturance is essential to brain development and the integration of brain regulatory systems. Infants are active participants in nurturing relationships.

Mirror neurons, active shortly after birth, promote empathic attunement between infant and caregiver. Healthy early relationships take advantage of brain plasticity, shaping the prefrontal cortex to make emotional regulation, prosocial behavior, and complex social decision making possible. These abilities are wisdom's components (Meeks and Jeste, 2009). Neglect and unhealthy bonds can be devastating. By age three, the individual social brain's basic neural substrate is set. Fortunately, psychological research has found an association between wisdom and resilience in the face of early life challenges (Hall, 2010).

Brain plasticity remains throughout life. The more experiences we have, the better our chances of becoming wise (Hall, 2010). Again, interpersonal biology explains plasticity and wisdom in relation to evolution and survival. According to Cozolino (2006) plasticity is necessary for developing new relationships, and as we mature, success in human relationships means our survival needs will continue to be met. Wisdom, a composite of relational abilities, is a long-term survival mechanism. Siegel (2010) has applied this knowledge therapeutically by creating a process that uses mindfulness practices, often associated with Zen Buddhism, as intervention to develop what he refers to as mindsight. Mindsight is a composite of positive characteristics of prefrontal cortex function, so this list of characteristics overlaps a great deal with the Meeks and Jeste (2009) list of components of wisdom. Siegel also includes intuition, a function of this brain area, on his list. The goal of mindsight mindfulness intervention is to transform the prefrontal cortex to promote integrative rewiring that supports emotional self-regulation and thoughtful action. The similarities between mindsight and wisdom are clear, although Siegel (2010) discusses wisdom only briefly.

Aging brains are naturalized by interpersonal biology. Cozolino (2006) explains that as brains age, they lose cortical cells, pruning away unused networks and increasing connectivity throughout what remains. Abilities change significantly. Older brains are more integrated across hemispheres, rather than being specialized. Cognitive processing is slower, but more parts of the brain are activated simultaneously. This is what neuropsychologist Goldberg (2006) refers to as a wisdom paradox: The brain is shrinking, losing processing speed and focus, while concurrently expanding its capacity for seeing the big picture and solving complex problems of living. Age-related changes manifest as improved comprehension of meaning and the tendency toward storytelling, making older adults better at teaching than learning, which Cozolino (2006) and Damasio (2010) suggest is perhaps an evolutionary selection to assist the transmission of cultural wisdom and advance the ongoing shaping of culture.

Wisdom: Seeking Sacred Reconnection

Is transcendent wisdom found through seeking on a spiritual path, as Harris (2009) suggests? Does it manifest in mystical experiences of unity, or experiences of the hidden wholeness? If the natural state of the mind is open mindful awareness, *prajna*, the beginning of wisdom, and we adopt practices to return our busy minds to that state, are we on a spiritual path? Is it possible all these activities are a search for reconnection with an ancient paradoxical consciousness that returns to us our sense of place in the natural world? What might be the evolutionary significance of any of this, and of transcendent wisdom? There are no empirical answers to these questions, only glimpses into others' lived experience that tickle my mind with curious pleasure as I move through life's physical challenges, trying to choose wisely and remain compassionate.

As remarkable as our embodied minds may be, they face a difficult challenge every time they attempt the shift from preconscious thought, where we spend most of our time, into the world of action. Damasio (2010) discusses this challenge and writes that it is very possible that cultural and religious rituals provide a jump-start to the brain's decision operations, moving it from preconscious reverie to movement. Rituals shape this movement into socially useful forms.

I am reminded of writings about the dance practices of indigenous African Diaspora religions. Yvonne Daniel (2005) writes of the dances for Oya, a female divinity with tornado-like energy, guardian of the cemetery. Daniel describes these dances as embodied wisdom, learned through imitation and intuition, letting go to connect with singers and drummers in changing cycles of rhythm that alter the energy being stirred—their ultimate purpose being transformation through the energy centers, leading to an embodied experience of intimate connection with Oya's divine wisdom. There are aspects of secret to the dance knowledge, but it exists to serve the community of participants, not the dancer alone.

Emotional responses, such as those employed in sacred dance, are integral to all aspects of religious cognition, from expressive prayer to solemn ritual, and they are processed in the frontal lobes, so "to the extent that religion involves emotion, it involves frontal lobe processes" (McNamara, 2001, p. 243). This is a new area of interest for religion scholars, particularly the emotions of fear and wonder (Fuller, 2007). While these scholars don't purport to study wisdom, the connection is clear. Throughout the Biblical book of Proverbs, a guide to attaining wisdom and living a virtuous life, we repeatedly find the words "fear of the Lord." In Psalm 111, considered a part of wisdom literature, we read "The fear of the Lord is the beginning of wisdom." In Islamic wisdom literature, which is mostly nonscriptural, fear of God is commended as an essential virtue (Renard, 1996).

While *fear* is one accurate translation of the Hebrew word *yarah*, it is also translated as awe, wonder, reverence, and right relationship (Ramer, 2010). For this reason, awe and wonder are often tied to wisdom. This divergent definition of wisdom is an intriguing, paradoxical blend of the possibility of both negative and positive emotion in one word . . . fear and wonder. Fear is a universal emotion in the language of biology, a cross-culturally recognizable survival mechanism, and emotional regulation of fear is a component of wisdom (Fuller, 2007; Meeks and Jeste, 2009). But what if wonder is the beginning of wisdom?

Wonder is a different sort of emotion. Summarizing the mostly theoretical research on wonder, Fuller (2007) defines wonder as a complex hybrid of the positive emotions, joy and interest. Less ancient than basic emotions and more highly evolved, wonder is unique in generating a diffuse rather than focused attention, enlarging our perceptual field and inspiring compassion. It causes a sense of mystery, trust, and belonging. It encourages us to approach and enables us to move beyond self-interest. The reader's attention is called to the noticeable overlap between these characteristics and the concepts of paradoxical consciousness, mindfulness, and wisdom. Closely aligned with other emotions that arise in the face of novelty and the unexpected, wonder is stimulated by looking upon a beautiful natural landscape, and motivates a quest for increased connection and belongingness (Fuller, 2007).

Interestingly, wonder is most often discussed in relation to nature. Sometimes the discussion is specifically religious, as with nature religions (Fuller, 2007). Taylor (2007) writes eloquently about the lived religion arising from experiences of daily life, one example being aquatic nature religion. He explains that this form of spirituality includes many outdoor activities that invoke a sense of wonder, awe, wholeness, harmony, and transcendence. Lived nature religion tends to involve a perception that nature is sacred in some way, making it worthy of care, and a feeling of belonging and connection to the earth. Could this be an expression of transcendent wisdom?

References to wonder also permeate more secular writing about the human/nature relationship. When Louv (2008) writes passionately about nature deficit disorder, his writing is redolent with examples of wonder and its significance for health. When he presents the sad predicament of a new generation of children for whom outdoor activity activates fear circuitry rather than wonder, it is clear that evolutionary rewiring is speeding along, further disrupting our sense of connection with Mother Earth, and perhaps transforming what it means to be wise.

Conclusion and Implications for Practice

This chapter has traveled through dense and little explored territory, unfamiliar to readers who do not regularly interact with science. It has tried to weave a tenuous web of wisdom scholarship, making tentative connections among empirical research in the social and natural sciences, neuroscience-based theorizing, and lived experiences sometimes associated with wisdom. This is not a linear trail, and perhaps the first lesson for anyone assuming that only linear positivism exists in science is that science revels in messiness as it moves its discourse forward using precise collections of evidence.

The practical lessons for adult educators who hope to educate for wisdom are quite simple. First, look to neuroscience to help inform the evolving understanding of wisdom. Second, understand brain plasticity while accepting the limitations of education in changing individual human brains. Every learner presents with a specific three-year-old's brain that has been re-wired in highly unique ways by that learner's lifetime of experiences. Adult learners might be in the midst of a serious rewiring that they can't control. It isn't enough to say that we value diversity; we must be wise and accept that people truly are exceedingly different, and with adult learners, perhaps the best expert on what needs to be learned is the learner.

Finally, in thinking pedagogically about how to teach in ways that promote neural integration of the prefrontal cortex to enhance the chances for emergent wisdom—remember that neuroscience is beginning to suggest that adaptation to our current constructed culture may not be wise in terms of long-term social brain survival (Damasio, 2010). One can enhance connectivity to the point of brain exhaustion, as military neuroscientists are beginning to discover as they push the envelope of multitasking and human/technology interface (Shanker and Richtel, 2011). We must continue to honor each learner's history of experiences while providing for new learning that is experiential. We should take our cue from embodied cognitive science and interpersonal neurobiology, developing ways to integrate mindfulness and integrative movement practices as core components of education. And we should reconsider our personal valuing of wonder as a source of connectedness, then return ourselves and our students to nature and the outdoors.

References

Behar, D. "Dawn of Human Matrilineal Diversity." *American Journal of Human Genetics Publication,* 2008. Retrieved January 20, 2011, from https://genographic.national geographic.com/genographic/lan/en/dawn.html

Berman, M. *Wandering God: A study in Nomadic Spirituality*. Albany, N.Y.: State University of New York Press, 2000.

Cozolino, L. *The Neuroscience of Human Relationships*. New York: W.W. Norton, 2006.

Damasio, A. *Self Comes to Mind: Constructing the Conscious Brain*. New York: Pantheon, 2010.

Daniel, Y. *Dancing Wisdom: Embodied Knowledge in Haitian Vodou, Cuban Yoruba, and Bahian Candomblé*. Chicago: University of Illinois Press, 2005.

Fuller, R. C. "Spirituality in the Flesh: The Role of Discrete Emotions in Religious Life." *Journal of the American Academy of Religion*, 2007, 75(1), 25–51.

Giordano, J., and Engebretson, J. "Neural and Cognitive Basis of Spiritual Experience: Biopsychosocial and Ethical Implications for Clinical Medicine." *Explore*, 2006, 2(3), 216–225.

Goldberg, E. *The Wisdom Paradox*. New York: Gotham, 2006.

Hall, S. H. *Wisdom: From Philosophy to Neuroscience*. New York: Knopf, 2010.

Harris, J. C. "Hagia Sophia (Divine Wisdom)." *Archives of General Psychiatry*, 2009, 66(4), 353–354.

Jacoboni, M. *Mirroring People: The New Science of How We Connect with Others.* New York: Farrar, Straus, and Giroux, 2008.

James, W. *The Varieties of Religious Experience.* London: Longman, Greens and Company, 1905.

Jeste, D. V., and Harris, J. C. "Wisdom: A Neuroscience Perspective." *JAMA*, 2010, 304(14), 1602–1603.

Johnson, S., and Taylor, K. (eds.). *Neuroscience and Adult Learning.* New Directions in Adult and Continuing Education, no. 110. San Francisco: Jossey-Bass, 2006.

Louv, R. *Last Child in the Woods: Saving Our Children From Nature Deficit Disorder.* Chapel Hill, N.C.: Algonquin, 2008.

McNamara, P. Religion and the Frontal Lobes. In Adresen, J. (ed.). *Religion in Mind: Cognitive Perspectives on Religious Belief, Ritual, and Experience* (pp. 237–256). Cambridge: Cambridge University Press, 2001.

Meeks, T. W., and Jeste, D. V. "Neurobiology of Wisdom: A Literature Overview." *Archives of General Psychiatry*, 2009, 66(4), 355–365.

Merriam, S., Caffarella, R., and Baumgartner, L. *Learning in Adulthood: A Comprehensive Guide.* (2nd ed.). San Francisco: Wiley, 2007.

Ramer, M. M. The Numinous Beginning of Wisdom, 2010. Retrieved January 20, 2011, from   www.chicagocommunitymennonite.org/worship/sermons/upload/thenuminousbeginningofwisdomoctober172010

Renard, J. *Seven Doors to Islam: Spirituality and the Religious Life of Muslims.* Berkeley: University of California Press, 1996.

Shanker, T., and Richtel, M. "In New Military, Data Overload Can Be Deadly," in *Your Brain On Computers*, 2011. Retrieved January 18, 2011, from http://www.nytimes.com/2011/01/17/technology/17brain.html?pagewanted=1&_r=1&nl=todaysheadlines&emc=tha2

Siegel, D. J. *Mindsight: The New Science of Personal Transformation.* New York: Bantam, 2010.

Taylor, B. "Focus Introduction: Aquatic Nature Religion." *Journal of the American Academy of Religion*, 2007, 75(4), 863–874.

Varela, F. J., Thompson, E., and Rosch, E. *The Embodied Mind: Cognitive Science and Human Experience.* Boston: MIT, 1991.

ANN L. SWARTZ *is an instructor of nursing and an affiliate assistant professor of adult education at Penn State University–Harrisburg.*

3

This chapter invokes the spirit of Sophia *as metaphorical guide and describes a path for educators and practitioners that can assist in the recovery of wisdom in the face of increasing pressures of measurable outcomes within the field of lifelong learning.*

Searching for Sophia: Adult Educators and Adult Learners as Wisdom Seekers

Wilma Fraser, Tara Hyland-Russell

"It's real, you see," they said; "it's so much more real than the stuff we normally deliver." These words encapsulated the enthusiastic responses of a number of adult educators and trainers who attended a workshop offered as part of a larger conference on the future of adult/lifelong learning by Wilma's Department of Post-Compulsory Education and Training at her university in the United Kingdom in 2009. Wilma (Author 1) was one of the organizers:

> I was also giving a presentation, and was surprised when I entered the room that it was already full, with others at the door asking if I "could just squeeze another in." To many of the participants our names meant nothing; my session's success was due to my title: *Wisdom and Adult Learning.*

The room was, quite simply, bursting, both with numbers and with anticipation. The session went well; Wilma drew energy from the expectation of the crowd and generated an atmosphere that beat its own rhythm between input, discussion, exploration, and analysis. Wilma showed a picture of the two hands in Michelangelo's *Creation of Adam* (Figure 1) from the Sistine Chapel and asked participants to reflect on what exactly was being passed from God to Man in that iconic, forever-held moment of connection. Wilma revealed the rest of the picture—and the woman in God's embrace. Eve? Surely not, at the moment of Adam's genesis; then who might she be?

Art historians Hall and Steinberg (1993) argue this figure to be none other than the feminized personification of wisdom (*sapientia*), also known as *Sophia*, and her half-hidden nature reveals much about her contested

NEW DIRECTIONS FOR ADULT AND CONTINUING EDUCATION, no. 131, Fall 2011 © 2011 Wiley Periodicals, Inc.
Published online in Wiley Online Library (wileyonlinelibrary.com) • DOI: 10.1002/ace.418

Figure 1. Michelangelo's Creation of Adam (http://www.italian-renaissance-art.com/Sistine-Ceiling.html).

presence in prevailing Western discourses. This argument is supported by theologian Karen Armstrong, who notes:

> In the third century BCE, a Jewish writer personified the Wisdom of God that had brought the world into being. He imagined her at God's side, like Plato's demiourgo (2009, p. 79).

In the days following Wilma's presentation, three participants told her how they had incorporated the teaching of wisdom within their own tutor training sessions—gratifying to hear at the very least, but especially within the tutors' contexts: training bricklayers, Royal Engineers within the Army, and members of the police academy. Wilma's colleagues explained that they had felt impelled to take a risk: They wanted to share some of the energy created in the conference, but they could not have anticipated the welcome with which their words of wisdom were greeted by their student tutors.

This chapter explains the genesis of such enthusiasm in an effort to understand what inspired those participants to seek a flame and draw on its light to illuminate some of the shadows of their own teaching practices. We invoke the spirit of *Sophia* as metaphorical guide for an ongoing reclamation of wisdom spaces and heed her challenge to current articulations of, and emphases upon, skills and competence-based outcomes, which we believe are constricting our teaching and learning spaces. Our working definition of wisdom is a stance of openness, embracing possibility and multidimensionality. Wisdom is broader in scope than cognitive knowing and includes aspects of the sacred, divine, intuitive, and experiential. Our notion of wisdom finds echo in the words of Csikszentmihalyi and Rathunde (1990), who stress the paradoxical nature of wisdom's pursuit:

New Directions for Adult and Continuing Education • DOI: 10.1002/ace

> What all the ancient thinkers seemed to realize is that without wisdom, ways
> of knowing are constrained by a tragic paradox: the clearer the view they pro-
> vide, the more limited the slice of reality they reveal (p. 29).

In other words, we argue that many of our educational processes are so limited by outcome-based imperatives that we are in danger of limiting education's potential for multidimensional and real learning. As Jarvis reminds us:

> It is generally recognised that (the word education) may be derived from
> either one of two Latin words, "educare" or "educere": the first means "to
> train" which implies to prepare a person to take their place within the struc-
> tures of society, while the second means to "draw out," which places more
> emphasis upon the person and the process (as cited in Fraser, 1995, p. 43).

We urge the reclamation of that second emphasis on the person and the process. To reduce the purpose of education to the training needs of the market place lays waste to our opportunities for growth, transformation, and wisdom. Our thesis is based on a belief that we must challenge those taken-for-granted skills-based emphases that underpin so many of our current teaching practices, so that we can nourish the kind of openness and drawing out that fosters wisdom.

We first examine wisdom within adult learning paradigms. Next, we explore key metaphors of knowledge and wisdom which leads to a third section on conceiving wisdom spaces and then conclude with the implications for adult education.

Wisdom Within Adult Learning Paradigms

Writings on wisdom within adult learning paradigms have tended to draw upon psychological accounts that emphasize a developmental model embracing life's trajectories. Edmondson (2005) notes:

> It is among psychologists (rather than philosophers or sociologists) that
> research during the last quarter-century has re-focused on wisdom as uniting
> forms of intelligence that are acquired and developed during the lifecourse.
> This work echoes ancient approaches to practice-oriented forms of wisdom,
> and has seen thought, feeling, morality and experience as combined in wise
> discourse and decisions (p. 343).

The emphasis on wisdom's path over the lifecourse has led, in turn, to recent work on wisdom and gerontology (Randall and Kenyon, 2004) which draws upon narrative framings and assumptions similar to those discussed in adult education (Rossiter and Clark, 2007). Indeed, this is in line with many cross-cultural constructions of the wise elder or sage. However, such constructions rely, as Edmondson (2005) suggests, on the integration of "thought, feeling, morality and experience as combined in wise discourse and decisions" (p. 343).

What we are arguing in this chapter is that the potential for such integration, and therefore for wisdom, is itself based upon the kinds of discourses within which thought, feeling, morality, and experience are articulated and explored. And it is our contention that educational discourses are being reduced to mainly emphasize forms of knowledge that lead to economic competitiveness and not to wisdom. Trowbridge's (2007) analysis of major policy reports in the UK on lifelong education supports this view and he notes that, despite the rhetoric about lifelong learning, "There is little social support for accomplishing tasks such as deepening self-knowledge, achieving ego-integration and -transcendence, and gaining wisdom" (p. 165). The paucity of support for deepening self-knowledge has resulted in a reduction in formal education settings in the West that draw on integrated forms of knowledge that can lead to wisdom.

This is not to suggest, however, that education has been reduced to skills-based outcomes solely in response to economic factors. The pedagogical pursuit of wisdom has not simply fallen foul of "the relentless tendency to reduce education's purpose to employability" (West, 2010, p. 328). On the contrary, Edmondson (2005) views the contemporary demise of wisdom spaces as due to an increasingly less relevant religious worldview for the majority of people and a cognitive model of psychology that dominated the 20th century. To this we would add the shift in emphasis towards greater attention upon reason and rationality, what Dirkx (2001) calls the "rationalist doctrine" (p. 63). This shift in emphasis towards reason and away from faith arose in part during the Enlightenment period and was accompanied by diminished attention to the deeper meanings that our souls and spirits might seek and by increased attention on "factual information and the use of reason and reflection to learn from experience" (Dirkx, 2001, p. 63). Such deeper meaning, we argue, requires thought that is both complex and integrated—thought that cannot be packaged as items of skill-sets but that is imaginative and metarational. But how might we encourage such a shift in attention, which could assist in the recovery of wisdom and in the spaces where *Sophia* might be nurtured, nourished, and encouraged? How do we develop teaching practices where wisdom stories might be told and heard? Part of the answer is found in the language we choose for our teaching practices.

Metaphors of Knowledge and Wisdom

Metaphors profoundly shape our language and the ways in which we perceive the world. Hill and Johnston (2003) go so far as to assert that "reflecting on the effects of the language choices we make as adult educators is perhaps a deceptively simple *yet the most transformative action to undertake*"

(p. 21, italics added). It is likely because of its deceptively simple nature that we often disregard the ways that our language use shapes our theories, our ways of becoming as people and teachers, and our teaching practices. Metaphor is a powerful tool, and once we acknowledge that power, we can begin to see how the nature of the language that describes our current educational discourses can have such limiting effects. As Abbs (1979) cogently argued over thirty years ago:

> The instrumental view of education is recorded faithfully in the mechanical metaphors and grey abstractions of current educational discourse . . . The effect of such language is to numb the mind . . . It is not an accident that many of the metaphors, dead as they are, derive from mechanics . . . from military manoeuvres . . . and from behavioural psychology . . . It is the language of stasis, leaving education without a subject, without a history and without a future (pp. 11–12).

The gray, static language of mechanics and military is a far cry from the dynamic potential for meaning-making that we see inscribed in our image of *Sophia*. For us, *Sophia* offers resonance, energy, and potential: "She is, in fact, the learning process itself. She calls us to a life of seeking understanding of the world in which we live" (Cole, Ronan, and Taussig, 1996, p. 23).

Metaphors actively forge connections between our inner, personal meanings and the outer contexts in which we live our lives. The theoretical models we use not only inform our thoughts but actively shape our behavior and practice. According to Richardson (1997), "We become the metaphors we use. We construct worlds in our metaphoric image" (p. 185). This is our challenge as adult educators: If we want learning to offer transformation, energy, and a future, we must find ways to engage our students in vibrant metaphors of learning that provide multiple options and growth for both educator and learner and that animate perceptions of learning as active and agential.

Spiral as Generative Metaphor of Wisdom. As an outgrowth of the metaphorical image of *Sophia* as wisdom, we concur with others (Kegan, 1982; Bateson, 1994; Tisdell, 2003) in suggesting the spiral as a generative metaphor of development. As Tara (Author 2) has discussed elsewhere (Hyland-Russell, 2001), the spiral nautilus can be a profound metaphor for the deepening awareness and integration of one's personal, relational, and cultural stories. The spiral nautilus shell is constructed as a series of chambers that lead deeper into further chambers, spiralling around the inner self. Yet the chambers also open outward, connecting the inner creature with the surrounding sea. Using a spiral metaphor for wisdom learning processes provides a model through which to evaluate and mediate among conflicting discourses and social pressures, not least of which are the current economic paradigms, and values the wisdom that emerges from one's personal and communal journey. Here we find an echo with the work of feminist theologian

Catherine Keller, for whom wisdom "at least as practised in the indigenous and biblical traditions, is irredeemably implicated in the sensuous, the communal, the experiential, the metanoic, the unpredictable, the imaginal, the practical" (in Deane-Drummond, 2007, p. 176).

"Waiting on" as Metaphor for Wisdom. Not only literal and metaphorical spaces facilitate the development of wisdom but also the attitudes in which we approach learning. Our pedagogical stances have great capacity to foster the kinds of spaces in our classes where aspects of "our [and *our students'*] unique wisdom stories" (Randall and Kenyon, 2004, p. 342) can be nourished and encouraged. Urging alternatives to the heavy certainties that characterize much adult learning and teaching, we suggest, instead, the kind of careful attentiveness so evocatively captured by McGilchrist (2009):

> The stance, or disposition, that we need to adopt, according to Heidegger, is one of "waiting on" (*nachdenken*) something, rather than just "waiting *for*" it; a patient, respectful nurturing of something into disclosure, in which we need already to have some idea of what it is that will be. George Steiner compares it to "that 'bending toward' of spirit and intellect and ear" to be seen in Fra Angelico's *Annunciation* in San Marco (p. 152).

It is this sense of attentiveness that we also want to encourage in our classroom practices. We urge the fostering of environments where *Sophia* might find welcome and expression: a *waiting on* wisdom that both creates an expectation in teachers and students for wisdom and actively shapes their learning practices to make wisdom possible.

We see a certain irony, here, in Michaelangelo's placing of the female figure in the *Creation of Adam*. If we concur with Hall and Steinberg (1993) and their suggestion that she is the personification of wisdom, her framing within this section of the painting has always been overshadowed by the iconic image of God's hand linking with Adam's. Perhaps it is time that wisdom came out of the shadow of God's embrace and claimed her place at the heart of the educative process.

Conceiving Wisdom Spaces

We need to conceive and foster the physical, mental, emotional, and moral spaces for wisdom learning. Deane-Drummond (2007) draws from Aquinas' notion of practical wisdom to suggest wisdom-infused learning that is oriented toward the common good and that fosters *citizen virtues*, an active and full responsibility to family and the public sphere. How then can we both imagine and sustain spaces that support learners in their pursuit of introspection, reflexivity, and the development of wisdom? Each of us offers an example from our own practice.

New Directions for Adult and Continuing Education • DOI: 10.1002/ace

Wisdom in the Radical Humanities. In a study of Canadian *Radical Humanities* programs for marginalized nontraditional adult learners, Tara and her research partner Janet Groen argue for the "power of humanities education to create a reflective space in which students can develop critical thinking capacities" (Groen and Hyland-Russell, 2010, p. 39). This reflective space is far less common than the short-term vocational or training programs usually prescribed for low-income people (Cunningham, 1993) but also is far more effective in promoting the kinds of metarational thinking and imaginative consideration of self in relation to the world associated with wisdom-seeking. Though it would be reasonable to assume that low-income or homeless people need, first and foremost, practical skills to escape poverty, Tara's experience teaching, administering, and researching *Radical Humanities* programs has instead shown the value of a wisdom approach.

Time and again the marginalized adult learners report their previous referrals to yet another skills-based program intended to lead them out of poverty: budgeting, computer skills, or job retraining. Yet, despite their willing, if not eager, participation, the low-income learners did not find any appreciable benefit to the skills-based programs. To their amazement, however, when exposed to studies of ethics, history, or literature through one of the *Radical Humanities* programs, they began to evaluate their values against social norms and to assess the structural mechanisms that had impoverished them. They were able to imagine new possibilities for their lives based on the stories of self and other in relation to the metaphorical worlds that they encountered through the humanities. Students found far more freedom through engaging in the dialogic space of the humanities than they did in upskilling programs designed to liberate them from poverty. In the words of one participant, "skills-based programs don't require critical engagement, but memorization of tasks. Humanities involves your whole self and requires thinking about how your viewpoint and life relate to others and the world. It makes us think of things we couldn't imagine before" (Tracy Ray). Participants' experiences suggest that real and transformative learning comes not from mastering another set of narrowly defined skills, but from an ongoing process that actively integrates private and public, known and experienced, practical and imaginative.

Wisdom and Adult Learning. We began this chapter with reference to Wilma's workshop on Wisdom and Adult Learning. One of those participants celebrated the challenge that the session presented and shared his applied insights with Wilma as part of Wilma's current research into wisdom and adult learning. John retired from the police force after thirty years' service and attaining the position of Detective Chief Superintendent. He now teaches within the Department of Post Compulsory Education and Training at Canterbury Christ Church University (United Kingdom), where his roles include national teacher-training for the police force. He talks of the environment that pervaded the police service before he left and connected that environment with the current situation in adult education:

A lot of the issues were the management mantras . . . "value for money," "effi-
ciencies," "economies," "more for the same" and "the same for less" and it
appeared to me that we were actually beginning to lose focus from what we
were here to do and we very much got into instrumentalist sort of policies,
and works, and targets and performance which skewed a lot of the real purpose of policing. But the thing that surprised me is that some of the things
that I railed against in the police force, I still rail against today [in education]
because the aims and objectives, the intended learning outcomes, the lesson
planning is so defined they've actually lost the plot of what they're here to do.

As an antidote to the prevailing loss of focus, John now includes Wilma's
slide of Michelangelo's *Creation of Adam*, and for every cohort of learners, he
posits wisdom as an alternate way of learning and teaching. When Wilma
asked John how he defined wisdom, he illustrated wisdom teaching by
describing how a trainee tutor he was observing had been adhering closely
to the mandatory lesson plan and then abruptly shifted to respond to the students and offer a more open stance by illustrating the lesson through her
own experience. "Halfway through the lesson she binned it and she told a
story—she told a story of her own experience that related to the subject . . .
and she had those people in the palm of her hand and so much learning took
place and it's that sort of thing that I think is wisdom" (John). Of course,
John is not suggesting that simple storytelling is all that is needed for *Sophia*
to take her place center-stage; rather, he is noting the importance of placing
the story within the felt experience of the teaching/learning exchange. While
this might appear as no more than common sense, John's argument, and ours
in this chapter, is that too much of our educational practice is increasingly
confined within the restrictive metaphorical world of the skills-based marketplace. Such limitation will, inevitably, restrict the imaginal spaces within
which the seeds of deeper learning might grow and mature.

Conclusion

We believe that it is indeed possible to create wisdom spaces in adult education, in spite of the pressure to have measurable outcomes. Burdened by
what we perceive to be a profound disjunction between the delivery of packaged units of learning and the opening of the mind and soul to greater
knowing that cannot always be predicted, we posit a view of wisdom that
concurs with Abbs's definition of "Education [as] to do with educing, with
releasing, with liberating" (1994, p. 15). The emerging work in Adult Education on spirituality and authenticity is encouraging theoretical and pedagogical spaces for *Sophia* to enter the classroom. We can pay heed to the
metaphors and discourses we use in our teaching, research, and scholarship:
We can deliberately choose language that resonates with the possibilities of
intuition and wisdom, rather than relying on reductive metaphors relating

New Directions for Adult and Continuing Education • DOI: 10.1002/ace

to the marketplace. Thus, the very act of invoking or inviting *Sophia* into our educational discourses can confront and speak back to the power of the prevailing and limiting narrative framings.

Central to our endeavors, and crucial to any criterion for success, we must also strive to confront the mindnumbing limitations of our current pedagogical emphasis on certainties and outcomes. We urge, in contrast, an attitude of attentiveness and encouragement towards the potential for unknowing as both antidote and opportunity for change: We can "wait upon" *Sophia* through our attitudes. We need to reclaim the circle, the spiral, and learn to tolerate the uncertain, the unknown, the unpredictable. As Edmondson notes, "It is a perennial feature of wisdom . . . that it eschews dogmatism or certitude" (2005, p. 342). If instrumentalist, consumerist, or bureaucratic forms of rationality become dominant rationales for social worldviews, the idea that a life should in any way make sense becomes less and less of a possibility. And it is because of its power to help a life become meaningful that the pursuit of wisdom is so crucial. We are reminded of the poet Keats's urging for the ability to live in "negative capability, that is when a man (sic) is capable of being in uncertainties, mysteries, doubts, without any irritable reaching after fact and reason" (from a letter to his brothers dated December 21, 1817, quoted in *The Cambridge Guide to Literature in English*, Ian Ousby, ed., p. 672). Paradoxically, we are more likely to encounter the wisdom of *Sophia* if we are willing to abandon rational certitude and embrace a stance of curiosity and openness, what we could call "unknowing." We ignore *Sophia*'s call at our peril:

> You who are waiting for me, take me to yourselves.
>
> And do not banish me from your sight.
>
> And do not make your voice hate me, nor your hearing.
>
> Do not be ignorant of me anywhere or any time. Be on
>
> your guard!
>
> (Hymn of praise to *Sophia*, from The Nag Hammadi Library, in Simon, 2004, p. 222)

References

Abbs, P. *Reclamations: Essays on Culture, Mass-Culture and the Curriculum.* London: Heinemann, 1979.

Abbs, P. *The Educational Imperative.* Washington, D.C.: The Falmer Press, 1994.

Armstrong, K. *The Case for God.* London: The Bodley Head, 2009.

Bateson, M. *Peripheral Visions: Learning Along the Way.* New York: HarperCollins, 1994.

Cole, S., Ronan, M., and Taussig, H. *Wisdom's Feast: Sophia in Study and Celebration.* Kansas City: Sheed and Ward, 1996.

Csikszentmihalyi, M., and Rathunde, K. "The Psychology of Wisdom: An Evolutionary Interpretation." In R. Sternberg (ed.), *Wisdom: Its Nature, Origins, and Development*. Cambridge, U.K.: Cambridge University Press, 1990.

Cunningham, P. "Let's Get Real." *Adult Education Quarterly*, 1993, 22,3–15.

Deane-Drummond, C. "Wisdom Remembered: Recovering a Theological Vision of Wisdom for the Academe." *London Review of Education*, 2007, 5, 173–184.

Dirkx, J. "The Power of Feeling: Emotion, Imagination, and the Construction of Meaning in Adult Learning." In S. B. Merriam (ed.), *The New Update on Learning Theory*. New Directions for Adult and Continuing Education, no. 89. San Francisco: Jossey-Bass, 2001, 63–72.

Edmondson, R. "Wisdom in Later Life: Ethnographic Approaches." *Ageing and Society*, 2005, 25, 339–356.

Fraser, W. *Learning from Experience: Empowerment or Incorporation?* Leicester, U.K.: NIACE, 1995.

Groen, J., and Hyland-Russell, T. "Riches from the Poor: Teaching Humanities in the Margins." In M. Alfred (ed.), *Learning for Economic Self-Sufficiency*. Charlotte, N.C.: Information Age, 2010.

Hall, M., and Steinberg, L. "Who's Who in Michelangelo's Creation of Adam?" *The Art Bulletin*, 1993, 75, 340–344.

Hill, L., and Johnston, J. "Adult Education and Humanity's Relationship with Nature Reflected in Language, Metaphor, and Spirituality: A Call to Action." In L. H. Hill and D. E. Clover (eds.), *Environmental Adult Education: Ecological Learning, Theory, and Practice for Socioenvironmental Change*. New Directions for Adult and Continuing Education, no. 99. San Francisco: Jossey-Bass, 2003, 17–26.

Hyland-Russell, T. "The Storied Nautilus: Life Writing, Narrative Therapy and Women's Self-Storying." Unpublished doctoral dissertation, Department of English, University of Calgary, 2001.

Kegan, R. *The Evolving Self: Problems and Process in Human Development*. Cambridge, Mass.: Harvard University Press, 1982.

McGilchrist, I. *The Master and his Emissary: The Divided Brain and the Making of the Western World*. New Haven, Conn.: Yale University Press, 2009.

Ousby, I. (ed). *The Cambridge Guide to Literature in English*. Cambridge: Cambridge, 1993.

Randall, W., and Kenyon, G. "Time, Story, and Wisdom: Emerging Themes in Narrative Gerontology." *Canadian Journal on Aging*, 2004, 23, 333–346.

Richardson, L. *Fields of Play: Constructing an Academic Life*. New Brunswick, N.J.: Rutgers, 1997.

Rossiter, M., and Clark, M. *Narrative and the Practice of Adult Education*. Malabar, Fla.: Krieger, 2007.

Simon, B. *The Essence of the Gnostics*. London: Arcturus Publishing Limited, 2004.

Tisdell, E. *Exploring Spirituality and Culture in Adult and Higher Education*. San Francisco: Jossey-Bass, 2003.

Trowbridge, R. "Wisdom and Lifelong Learning in the Twenty-First Century." *London Review of Education*, 2007, 5, 159–172.

West, L. "A Contrasting World: Adult Education and Lifelong Learning, History and Life History in the Study of Adult Learning." *Looking Back, Looking Forward: Learning, Teaching and Research in Adult Education Past, Present and Future*. Proceedings of 40th Annual Conference (Standing Conference on University Teaching and Research in the Education of Adults). University of Warwick, 2010.

WILMA FRASER *is a principal lecturer of post-compulsory education at Canterbury Christ Church University, England, U.K.*

TARA HYLAND-RUSSELL *is an associate professor of English at St. Mary's University College, Calgary, Alberta, Canada.*

New Directions for Adult and Continuing Education • DOI: 10.1002/ace

This chapter offers an overview of research on wisdom and strategies that educators can employ to foster the development of wisdom in themselves and in their students; it presents the view that it is practical wisdom that helps us get through difficult situations in ways that enhance our common humanity.

Understanding and Teaching Practical Wisdom

Caroline L. Bassett

One day in the summer of 2010 at a baseball game, a pitcher was throwing a perfect no-hitter, but at the bottom of the ninth inning, the umpire called the batter safe at first base, when replays showed that, in fact, he was out. Did the pitcher stomp over to the umpire, yell in his face, throw his glove on the ground, swear, and turn red with fury? No. Instead, the umpire, Jim Joyce, personally apologized to the pitcher Armando Galarraga, saying that he was wrong in the Detroit Tigers–Cleveland Indians baseball game on June 2, 2010 (Kepner, 2010). Further, in a number of interviews, Joyce publicly acknowledged his mistake. Galarraga said that he told the umpire, "Nobody's perfect."

Some might argue that the behavior of either of these men is not wisdom. I, however, claim that it indicates wisdom or suggests it. For either the pitcher or the umpire, a pattern of such behaviors would point to the possible presence of wisdom because wisdom is a habit of thinking and behaving that helps us get through difficult interpersonal situations in ways that work well for most who are involved. When two women appeared before King Solomon claiming to be the mother of the same baby, he called for the child to be cut in two, one half for each of them. One of the women cried out not to kill it and to give it to the other woman. King Solomon awarded the child to the weeping woman, recognizing that she was the true mother. On a more contemporary and larger scale, in South Africa the Truth and Reconciliation Commission was established in 1995 to help the country deal with the abuses perpetrated by all parts of society during apartheid (www.justice.gov.za/trc/). This was a wise move that prevented further violence.

NEW DIRECTIONS FOR ADULT AND CONTINUING EDUCATION, no. 131, Fall 2011 © 2011 Wiley Periodicals, Inc.
Published online in Wiley Online Library (wileyonlinelibrary.com) • DOI: 10.1002/ace.419

I offer the baseball story as an example of wisdom, practical everyday wisdom, in which human nature is recognized and accepted for what it is, no one makes a fuss, a mistake is gracefully acknowledged, and life goes on. We tend to think of wisdom as something almost unattainable for most of us, difficult to achieve or even approach, the "pinnacle or hallmark of adult thinking" (Merriam, Caffarella, and Baumgartner, 2007, p. 351), a Mount Everest of human attainment. A few reach those lofty heights at some times during their lives, making decisions with far-reaching implications that bring about positive change. I am thinking of, for example, Jesus, Abraham Lincoln, and Wangari Maathai, the Nobel Peace Prize winner from Kenya with her contribution to sustainable development, democracy, and peace.

It is, however, misleading to think of wisdom as an exalted and all-but-unattainable quality that only a few highly developed people achieve. Actually, most of us have some wisdom within us that we can use on a daily basis, especially if we work explicitly towards that end. Our scope will not encompass so much as that of the more public figures, but it is my belief that any of us (or at least most of us) can learn the skills and abilities associated with wisdom and practice them in daily life.

Based on my understanding, my definition of wisdom is as follows: *Wisdom is about human flourishing; it is having sufficient awareness in various situations and contexts to act in ways that enhance our common humanity.* This definition provides a base for the rest of this chapter, which will provide a brief overview of what we know about wisdom from the literature, three formulations to help us understand wisdom better, and finally recommendations for practice for adult educators.

Wisdom: What We Know

Because wisdom is such a complex and multidimensional construct (Holliday and Chandler, 1986), it is difficult to study, much less to define. Nevertheless—or because of that—people in a range of fields such as psychologists (Sternberg, 1990; Baltes and Staudinger, 1993), sociologists (Ardelt, 2003), management professors (Gibson, 2008), neuroscientists (Meeks and Jeste, 2009), and adult educators (Jarvis, 1992, 2004; Bassett, 2006), to name just a few, are investigating it. (For a more complete discussion, see Bassett, 2006.)

Three main schools of thought have produced their understanding of wisdom. Sternberg's (1990, 2001) work centers around his balance theory, in which balancing different interests and tasks can lead to the common good. The Berlin School (Baltes and Staudinger, 1993) sees wisdom as "expert knowledge in the fundamental pragmatics of life permitting exceptional insight, judgment, and advice involving complex and uncertain matters of the human condition" (p. 76). Finally, through her empirical research, Ardelt (2003, 2004) has developed a three-dimensional wisdom scale that includes cognitive, affective, and reflective dimensions. Other approaches

New Directions for Adult and Continuing Education • DOI: 10.1002/ace

find wisdom to be an aspect of postformal development, such as, in an older study Orwoll and Perlmutter's (1990) discussion of self-transcendence being part of wisdom, where a person can move "beyond individualistic concerns to more collective or universal ones" (p. 162). On the other hand, Yang (2008) argues that wisdom is a real-life process that can be used in everyday situations. Actually, these last two concepts are not contradictory, because holding a more universalistic standpoint does not preclude applying it to ordinary situations, which is what I would argue.

Ardelt's (2003) is not the only instrument that attempts to measure wisdom, though hers, the 3D-WS (Three-Dimensional Wisdom Scale), is perhaps the soundest and most robust from a research point of view. It measures cognitive, reflective, and affective behaviors, with reflection being the core of the process of wisdom, from which the other two arise. Her sample includes older adults. Although most researchers agree that wisdom comes from age and experience, Brown and Greene (2006) studied younger adults, using 1,188 college students in an instrument that they designed and called the Wisdom Development Scale. It showed six validated factors of wisdom: self-knowledge, emotional management, altruism, inspirational engagement, judgment, and life knowledge.

A third very recent research project used a two-phase Delphi method study to understand the characteristics of wisdom. Based on a consensus panel of twenty-seven international wisdom experts, the findings show considerable agreement among them that wisdom appears to be a distinct entity that differs from both intelligence and spirituality and includes domains such as "practical application of knowledge, use of knowledge for common social good, and integration of affect and knowledge" (Jeste and others, 2010, p. 671). The authors, at least three of whom are psychiatrists, suggest that wisdom "is a uniquely human but rare personal quality which can be learned and measured and increases with age through advanced cognitive *and* [emphasis in original] emotional development that is experience-driven. At the same time, wisdom is not expected to increase by taking medication" (p. 678).

For educators, since we can't buy the pills for ourselves and our students, how do we teach wisdom, or wisdom-related skills? How do we support the advanced cognitive and emotional development necessary for the growth of wisdom in the people in our worlds, both in the classroom and for those around us? To address these questions, I am postulating three formulations on wisdom that are based on my research and the literature.

Three Formulations of Wisdom

Here are three formulations on understanding wisdom.

1. Wisdom Can Be Understood as the Integration and Interaction of Several Elements. Based on a grounded theory study of twenty-four thoughtful, insightful people nominated by community leaders using the snowball method, I have developed the Dynamics of Wisdom model (which can be accessed at www.wisdominst.org). This model shows not only the components of wisdom and how they interact, but also suggests ways to cultivate our wisdom.

The major components of the model include the cognitive, affective, active, and reflective domains, each with associated proficiencies, all of which interact with each other. It is imperative to keep in mind that wisdom lies not in any one of them but rather in their interaction.

More particularly, in the cognitive domain we find discernment, objectivity, and holistic thinking. *Respect*, the affective domain, includes openness and acceptance, empathy, multiple-perspective-taking, and generosity of spirit. In *Engagement*, the active domain, we find involvement in the world and sound judgments based on fairness and justice. Finally, integrity is the principal characteristic of the *Reflection* domain, along with self-transcendence and seeing the self as part of complex systems, hence tolerating ambiguity and paradox. This model is actually a developmental spiral: the more a person develops self-transcendence, the more he or she can see clearly (be discerning); the more discerning a person is, the more likely he or she is to have an expanded sphere of consideration of who and what matters, so more is included in what has to be discerned and acted upon. The more individuals are involved in the world using sound judgment, the more discerning they need to be and the more there is to take into account when weighing alternatives. Each one of these domains affects the other.

Nor is the interaction of these elements that constitute wisdom without objective reference. In a recent review of the literature on wisdom and functional neuroimaging, Jeste and Harris (2010) found that two brain regions, the prefrontal cortex and the limbic striatum, are involved. They state that "wisdom seems to require the brain to carefully match and integrate the activities of these areas" (p. 1602).

2. Wisdom Lies on a Continuum. The aforementioned Jeste and Harris (2010) believe as I do that wisdom, like intelligence, lies on a continuum as a continuous construct, rather than being a categorical one that is either present or absent. This idea goes against conventional mainstream assumptions about wisdom—that people are wise or unwise. We think of Abraham Lincoln, Eleanor Roosevelt, or Nelson Mandela—they are the wise ones, and there is no way that we can match them in insight and perspicacity. Therefore, as we cannot attain this level of functioning, the all-or-nothing thinking goes, we don't have it and therefore believe that wisdom is not for us.

On the contrary, as Meeks and Jeste (2009) suggest, wisdom is a trait distributed across the population. This statement contradicts the findings of the Delphi expert panel (which these researchers were instrumental in designing and carrying out), which found, by consensus, that wisdom is rare. Perhaps it is both—it can exist incipiently across the population, but its full flowering is rare. If we see wisdom lying on a developmental continuum with that flowering at one end, exemplified by some of the people I have already mentioned, then along the middle we have ordinary people who may act wisely some of the time. We could say that their development in terms of emotional maturity and cognitive complexity lies in the moderate range. At the other end, we would find wisdom as prudence: if it looks like rain, it's a good idea to take an umbrella. Or, do not badmouth a former employee because you may be working with that person someday. Regular old common sense.

Does being developed mean that someone is wise? Not necessarily. Sternberg, Reznitskaya, and Jarvin (2007) caution us to remember that the ends of knowledge (and I would add, development) matter. Further, the scope or the impact of the wisdom differs depending on the context and the players. A student of mine was able to step back from her situation and come up with a solution in which she could help her daughter with newborn twins but yet not lose the recently won freedom she got with her retirement—she would provide some childcare at night and, at the same time, give the family money to hire help. It seems that she took a compromise route, rather than an either/or one, where she would have been annoyed at her daughter for asking too much and at herself for giving too much. Here, the scope is small compared to the influence of the Buddha, for example, or Martin Luther King Jr., whose role allowed his wisdom to have a broader impact.

3. Some People Have a Greater Propensity for Wisdom. In order to pitch a perfect game, the pitcher Armando Galarraga mentioned earlier, is obviously an excellent athlete. Near the other end of the scale, I once participated in a ten-kilometer run, finished near the end, and never did anything like that again. Renée Fleming at the Metropolitan Opera performs with superb technique and interpretation, while my friend participates in a local choral group—both sing, but what a difference. Thus, it seems that wisdom too may have its excellent performers and those who demonstrate it less well and less frequently.

Just as people differ in all kinds of ways in terms of personality, skills, and abilities, so too with wisdom. The concatenation of abilities that make up wisdom is more prevalent in some people than others, or put to better use, or done so more often. That is, some people have greater capacity in some areas of wisdom than in others, manifesting various components and subcomponents of wisdom better or more frequently. Jim is more easily able to take the point of view of another person (the affective component) while Jack can look at situations more objectively than Jim. With his holistic worldview, he can see causes and consequences with some accuracy (the cognitive domain). On the job, Judge Jane has to use her cognitive abilities and remain objective; at the same time, she makes judgments and takes actions based on fairness and justice in her professional and personal life (the active component). Then we have Joyce who is highly reflective, who can tolerate paradox and uncertainty, and who is rarely deluded by the demands of her ego, allowing her to see more clearly and be more discerning, which takes us back to the cognitive domain. While wiser people operate more out of one of the dimensions than the others, they use all the components to a greater or lesser degree when making decisions.

What creates these differing abilities, I cannot say—it leads to the question of why people differ from each other in all kinds of ways. I think that people born with a greater capacity in several of these components—if these several interact felicitously—have a greater possibility of acting wisely more of the time than others.

Fostering Wisdom and Learning

In this section I will review three attempts to foster wisdom with useful strategies and then provide more ideas on enhancing wisdom in ourselves and our students. In a course entitled "Wisdom as Skill" for retirees in New York State, Trowbridge (2007) had the participants engage in three different activities. First, they learned about wisdom itself through reading philosophical, religious, and psychological literature. Second, they strove to develop a wisdom perspective through practicing character traits associated with wisdom, such as empathy, openness, and fairness. Finally, to practice wisdom in real-life situations, they kept journals where they recorded their attempts at acting wisely and shared them with others.

In the second example, what matters is how you use knowledge. Sternberg, Reznitskaya, and Jarvin (2007) have proposed wisdom-related instruction in U.S. middle schools. (Many of these activities can serve adult learners too.) Using the vehicle of American history, they urge teachers to help students think dialectically and dialogically so that they can understand the vested interests of various participants in a situation from the point of view of an individual, other people (or peoples) in different roles in society, and institutions. They advocate getting students to think about how everything that they learn, and everything that is known, can be used for better or worse ends—and that the ends matter.

Finally, Glück and Baltes (2006) conducted a study in which they attempted to enhance the wisdom of 318 adult participants. Using short-term interventions, which included an evaluative component, they asked participants not what they would do when faced with a life problem but instead what a wise response to it would be. The authors concluded that a combination of three resources can increase wisdom: crystallized intelligence (the ability to use knowledge), life experience, and the personality-interface factor of Self-Regulation and Openness Toward Growth, and that the concept of wisdom "has a guiding quality only for individuals who have reached a certain developmental closeness to wisdom" (p. 688).

How can we as educators move our students (and ourselves) towards that developmental closeness to wisdom, further along the wisdom continuum? In addition to the previous suggestions, here are ten recommendations for practice.

1. *Use a perplexing problem or confounding quandary (a disorienting dilemma or experience with cognitive dissonance) to make the shift in perspective that wisdom seems to require.* The strategies of transformative learning can help with this shift. The Ontario Institute for the Study of Education defines transformational learning as "a deep structural shift in basic premises of thought, feelings, and actions . . . a shift in consciousness that dramatically and permanently alters our way of being in the world" (Morrell and O'Connor, 2002, p. xvii). The process starts with a problem—something that you can't make sense or meaning of— and includes four main steps: the experience itself, critical reflection on assumptions and biases, reflective discourse, and action (Mezirow, 2000). Daloz (2000) uses some of Mezirow's ideas and suggests four conditions for transformation: the presence of the Other, reflective discourse in a climate that is both supportive and challenging, a mentoring community, and opportunities for committed action. Both Dirkx (2006) on using the emotions and Cranton (2002) on reflective journals offer suggestions for working through the problem to a new understanding of self, the world, and the self in the world.

2. *Review strategies for living a life committed to the common good.* In another way to cultivate development, people can refer to the strategies discussed by Daloz, Keen, Keen, and Parks (1996). The authors interviewed more than 100 individuals to discover what motivated them towards committing to and working actively towards a common good, that they defined as ". . . individuals whose own well-being is inextricably bound up with the good of the whole" (p. 16). Some of their strategies include connection and complexity, community, compassion, and courage. One factor that contributed to this commitment was encounters with difference, not just diversity—for example, traveling to or living in a foreign country or visiting parts of your own country to which you would not ordinarily go and connecting in "constructive engagement with otherness" (Daloz, 2000, p. 110).

3. *Get to know the lives of the Nobel Peace Prize winners and others considered wise.* Surely this prize indicates a public acknowledgment of the presence of at least some wisdom. For example, recent winners include Mohammed Yunus, who established the Grameen Bank for microlending; Rigoberta Menchu, who prevented the genocide of her Qui'ché people in Guatemala; or Nelson Mandela, in his own book (1994) or in Daloz's (2000) illuminating reflections on him. How did they get to be the way they are?

4. *Include wisdom witnessing.* In my classes I ask the students to look around them for evidence of wisdom in daily life and report on it in the next session. It should become a habit of mind to be always on the lookout for wisdom. As for its opposite, manifoldly present folly or foolishness, I ask that they think of ways to turn the situation around into something wise, or at least wiser.

5. *Use role models and be one.* Find a role model in your life and examine how that person handles difficult situations. You can also act as a role model for wisdom in the classroom, as Sternberg, Reznitskaya, and Jarvin (2007) suggest, because what you do is more important than what you say.

6. *Honor experience by reflecting on it.* It is not enough to have experiences, because then all older people would be wise. Why aren't they? One ingredient to becoming wiser is reflection on what did and did not work in a difficult situation, whose interests were involved, and what the outcomes of different decisions might be.

7. *Make amends.* Take a hint from Alcoholics Anonymous for personal development. Although I know little about the program, and only from reading about it and hearing people talk about it, the process of making amends seems like one that demonstrates a certain amount of emotional maturity. One has to be able to acknowledge a wrong done to another and apologize for it (Alcoholics Anonymous, 2009).

8. *See everything as a story.* One way to help people see themselves more objectively is to encourage them to tell stories, their own stories, while understanding that their own story represents only one way of interpreting a situation. The Nigerian writer Chimamanda Adichie (2009) presents a passionate plea for relativistic seeing in her clip in www.ted.com/talks/chimamanda_adichie_the_danger_of_a_single_story.html

9. *Realize that hardly anything is only one thing.* By this, I mean that complexity and perhaps contradiction are inherent in almost any observation, thought, idea, or concept. Because it is hard to make categorical statements, don't try. Communicate complexity clearly.

10. *Keep your focus on what matters.* Wisdom is about what matters and what we do about it. Don't get distracted by surface symptoms in a difficult situation. Instead, look into the heart of the matter and do what you need to do.

Final Thoughts

It is my hope that we can include in our perspective on wisdom that it represents both the pinnacle of human development and also, as we travel along its continuum, part of the rough-and-tumble of life that helps us all move towards a common good for ourselves, for others around us, and for the planet from which we draw sustenance.

New Directions for Adult and Continuing Education • DOI: 10.1002/ace

References

Adichie, C. The Danger of a Single Story, TEDTalks, 2009. Retrieved July 30, 2010, from www.ted.com/talks/chimamanda_adichie_the_danger_of_a_single_story.html

Alcoholics Anonymous. *Twelve Steps and Twelve Traditions.* New York: Alcoholics Anonymous World Services, 2009.

Ardelt, M. "Empirical Assessment of a Three-Dimensional Wisdom Scale." *Research on Aging,* 2003, *25,* 275–324.

Ardelt, M. "Wisdom as Expert Knowledge System: A Critical Review of a Contemporary Operationalization of an Ancient Concept." *Human Development,* 2004, *7,* 257–285.

Baltes, P. B., and Staudinger, U. M. "The Search for a Psychology of Wisdom." *Current Directions in Psychology Science,* 1993, *2,* 75–80.

Bassett, C. "Laughing at Gilded Butterflies: Integrating Wisdom, Development, and Learning." In C. Hoare (ed.), *Handbook of Adult Development and Learning.* New York: Oxford University Press, 2006.

Brown, S. C., and Greene, J. A. "The Wisdom Development Scale: Translating the Conceptual to Concrete." *Journal of College Student Development,* 2006, *47,* 1–19.

Cranton, P. "Teaching for Transformation." In J. M. Ross-Gordon (ed.), *Contemporary Viewpoints on Teaching Adults Effectively.* New Directions for Adult and Continuing Education, no. 93. San Francisco: Jossey-Bass, 2002.

Daloz, L. "Transformative Learning for the Common Good." In J. Mezirow and Associates (eds.), *Learning as Transformation: Critical Perspectives on a Theory in Progress.* San Francisco: Jossey-Bass, 2000.

Daloz, L., Keen, C., Keen, F., and Parks, S. D. *Common Fire: Lives of Commitment in a Complex World.* Boston: Beacon Press, 1996.

Dirkx, J. "Engaging Emotions in Adult Learning: A Jungian Perspective on Emotion and Transformative Learning." In E. W. Taylor (ed.), *Teaching for Change.* New Directions for Adult and Continuing Education, no. 109. San Francisco: Jossey-Bass, 2006.

Gibson, P. S. "Developing Practical Management Wisdom." *Journal of Management Development,* 2008, *27*(5), 528–536.

Glück, J., and Baltes, P. "Using the Concept of Wisdom to Enhance the Expression of Wisdom Knowledge: Not the Philosopher's Dream but Differential Effects of Developmental Preparedness." *Psychology and Aging,* 2006, *21*(4), 679–690.

Holliday, S. G., and Chandler, M. J. *Wisdom: Explorations in Adult Competence.* Basel, Switzerland: Karger, 1986.

Jarvis, P. *Paradoxes of Learning: On Becoming an Individual in Society.* San Francisco: Jossey-Bass, 1992.

Jarvis, P. *Adult Education and Lifelong Learning: Theory and Practice.* New York: RoutledgeFalmer, 2004.

Jeste, D. V., Ardelt, M., Blazer, D., Kraemer, H. C., Vaillant, G., and Meeks, T. W. "Expert Consensus on Characteristics of Wisdom: A Delphi Method Study." *The Gerontologist,* 2010, *50*(5), 668–680.

Jeste, D. V., and Harris, J. C. "Wisdom—A Neuroscience Perspective." *Journal of the American Medical Association,* 2010, *304*(14), 1602–1603.

Kepner, T. "Perfect Game Thwarted by Faulty Call." *New York Times,* June 2, 2010.

Mandela, N. *Long Walk to Freedom.* Boston: Little, Brown, 1994.

Meeks, T. W., and Jeste, D. V. "Neurobiology of Wisdom." *Archives of General Psychiatry,* 2009, *66*(4), 355–365.

Merriam, S. B., Caffarella, R. S., and Baumgartner, L. M. *Learning in Adulthood: A Comprehensive Guide.* (2nd ed.) San Francisco: Jossey-Bass, 2007.

Mezirow, J. *Learning as Transformation: Critical Perspectives on a Theory in Progress.* San Francisco: Jossey-Bass, 2000.

Morrell, A., and O'Connor, M. A. "Introduction." In E. O'Sullivan, A. Morell, and M. A. O'Connor (eds.), *Expanding the Boundaries of Transformative Learning*. New York: Palgrave, 2002.

Orwoll, L., and Perlmutter, M. "A Study of Wise Persons: Integrating a Personality Perspective." In R. J. Sternberg (ed.), *Wisdom: Its Nature, Origins, and Development*. Cambridge, U.K.: Cambridge University Press, 1990.

Sternberg, R. J. (ed.) *Wisdom: Its Nature, Origins, and Development*. Cambridge, U.K.: Cambridge University Press, 1990.

Sternberg, R. J. "Wisdom and Education." *Perspectives in Education*, 2001, *19*(4), 1–16.

Sternberg, R. J., Reznitskaya, A., and Jarvin, L. "Teaching for Wisdom: What Matters is Not Just What Students Know, But How They Use It." *London Review of Education*, 2007, *5*(2), 143–158.

Trowbridge, R. H. "Wisdom and Lifelong Learning in the Twenty-First Century." *London Review of Education*, 2007, *5*(2), 159–172.

Yang, S.-y. "A Process View of Wisdom." *Journal of Adult Development*, 2008, *15*, 62–75.

CAROLINE L. BASSETT is the director of the Wisdom Institute (www.wisdominst.org) and teaches doctoral students at Walden University and Capella University.

5

This chapter discusses cross-cultural perspectives on wisdom as a process necessary to strive for a "good life" in a particular culture and what it means to educate adults in cross-cultural settings.

East Meets West: Cross-Cultural Perspectives on Wisdom and Adult Education

Shih-ying Yang

During my first year of graduate study in the United States in 1993, I attended an Asian students' gathering. When the conversation moved to cultural shock, we all gave examples of things we saw that shook our basic assumptions. One person mentioned how shocked she was when after the departmental dinner banquet, almost half of medical students went outside and smoked. This surprised me as well, and what I saw in this different culture made me much more aware of my own basic beliefs and assumptions: Knowledge helps people to pursue ideas about the good life and how to pursue and help others pursue it, but that does not necessarily translate into their own wise behavior. No doubt most of those students who engaged in such health-damaging behavior were still able to demonstrate expertise in their profession and served as excellent doctors when they graduated. Yet this experience still underlines for me how professional knowledge and training alone is not sufficient for living a good life, and the most educated are not necessarily the most wise.

Wisdom enables us to lead a good life (Assmann, 1994), as Baltes and Staudinger forcefully assert "wisdom is a key factor in the construction of a 'good life'" (2000, p. 124). Through wisdom, we discover many pathways to a good life for all (Sternberg, 1998). Although adult educators teach learners about a variety of subjects in different contexts, they do so partly to help them live meaningful and satisfying lives. Many topics discussed in adult education, such as praxis, reflection, learning from experiences, examining basic assumptions about life, and transformation of personal value and belief systems (Merriam, Caffarella, and Baumgartner, 2007), can help people to live

New Directions for Adult and Continuing Education, no. 131, Fall 2011 © 2011 Wiley Periodicals, Inc.
Published online in Wiley Online Library (wileyonlinelibrary.com) • DOI: 10.1002/ace.420

gratifying lives. For this reason, the pursuit of wisdom is an important goal for adult education, and adult education is important for developing wisdom in individuals and communities.

The good life for humankind is threatened by global warming, shortages of natural resources, cultural and religious conflicts, and financial crises, and therefore international cooperation is urgently needed to attain a good life for all. This grand purpose of adult education cannot be fully realized until adult educators embrace a diversity of cultural perspectives on wisdom and apply this understanding to their teaching.

This chapter is written for those who are interested in understanding and facilitating discussions of wisdom from different cultural perspectives. It is also written with the hope that a broadened cultural perspective can help practitioners in adult education settings interact with East Asian adult learners more successfully. Toward that end, the chapter begins by exploring differences between East and West cultural and intellectual traditions. The second part explores conceptions and manifestations of wisdom. Finally, it discusses implications for education in a cross-cultural context.

East/West Cultural and Intellectual Traditions

Conceptions of wisdom develop in a cultural context, which is affected by geography and local conditions (Geertz, 1973). Over time, different ways of life engender different worldviews. These worldviews in turn contribute to different conceptions of wisdom, education, and the pursuit of what it means to have a good life. Different cultures present us with different bases for what is termed "a good life" through human adaptation and survival. Understanding this reality not only enables us to broaden our own perspectives on other ideals of the good life but also helps us all to live better lives. This understanding also shapes intellectual traditions and psychological ways of relating, each of which affect conceptions of wisdom.

In considering the different traditions of the East and West, Nisbett (2003) notes, "more than a billion people in the world claim intellectual inheritance from ancient Greece and more than two billion are the heirs of ancient Chinese traditions of thought" (p. 1). To truly understand contemporary cultural differences of wisdom and education, it is important to consider the origins of these East/West differences.

Origins and Worldviews. Europe and Asia have vastly different natural environments. The ancient Greeks prospered in a coastal trading center in the eastern Mediterranean, which was the crossroads of the world. They constantly encountered other peoples who spoke different languages, had perplexing customs, and possessed utterly different notions about their world. Personal efforts to communicate and persuade were therefore valued in this environment (Nisbett, 2003).

In contrast, ancient Chinese civilization originated in a land-bound area near the great Yellow River, whose muddy flow has often caused devastating

New Directions for Adult and Continuing Education • DOI: 10.1002/ace

floods. The natural conditions were often not conducive to agriculture, so collective effort was essential for survival. Writing systems and standards of measurement were unified around 221 B.C. by the first emperor of the Chin Dynasty (Schirokauer, 1991). Thus, the ancient Chinese seldom encountered people whose customs and notions were radically different (Nisbett, 2003).

These different living conditions helped to form different worldviews. Nisbett (2003) suggests that the ancient Greeks conceived a world that consisted of independent objects with distinct qualities. They saw individuals as each having traits derived from these qualities. Everything in this world could be explained by underlying principles—logic and ultimate Truth. The fundamentals were not seen as changing with circumstances. Even ideas—the Forms—were seen as having a genuine reality and as existing in isolation from any particular context. Logical reasoning and precise analysis of the basics were the two best ways to understand the world.

By contrast, for the ancient Chinese, it was *Tao* or The Way—the natural force operating in a formless and holistic manner—that forms and guides the universe. Because everything in the universe is generated by the Tao, the Tao thus defies description, analysis, and categorization (Lao Tzu, 1963). The world so conceived is constantly changing and is full of contradictions and interconnections. This complex and ever-changing world cannot be completely understood by human efforts, which are better utilized to appreciate the world and harmonize with it (Chuang Tzu, 1964).

Effects in Traditional Educational Philosophy. These differing origins gave rise to different views of mind, emotion, and education that affected the development of East and West educational philosophies. The ancient Greeks believed that rationality is what distinguishes humans from animals. The human mind and body were thought to function independently, and the importance of the mind was emphasized over the importance of the body (Kaufmann and Baird, 1994). Abstract thinking and knowledge have value for their own sake. The knowledge of universal principles is closer to the Truth than the knowledge that concerns applications, which may vary according to particular conditions. In contrast, passions, which were thought to originate from the body, tended to interfere with the mind's function, and therefore were to be controlled and regulated (Cottingham, Stoothoff, and Murdoch, 1985). Gaining formal knowledge and developing intelligence thus became two major focuses of Western-style education.

The ancient Chinese believed that it is only in contexts and relationships that any comprehension of the world can be attained. Mind and body functions are inseparable (Chuang Tzu, 1964; Confucius, 1979). Cultivated affections, such as empathy, shame, humility, and tolerance, distinguish humans from animals (Mencius, 1970). Compassion and benevolence thus are more important human qualities than intelligence (Confucius, 1963a). Innate abilities can be made up by efforts (Stevenson and Stigler, 1992). Character cultivation and ethical conduct are the main focuses of Eastern education. Education involves learning how to be ethical beings or sages who can play different roles, fulfill different duties according to the changing contexts, and bring harmony to the world (Confucius, 1963b). Knowledge is valued for its pragmatic application to reap good results rather than as an end in itself. Action that carries out what is learned is an essential sign of true knowing (Chan, 1963). While educational philosophies are not quite so rigidly defined in our contemporary world, these traditional worldviews, growing out of the East and the West and influencing educational systems, still have contemporary effects. For example, contemporary Westerners live in a society in which the self is a unitary free agent, whereas contemporary East Asians live in an interdependent world in which the self is part of a larger whole (Triandis, 1995). This difference in perspective affects approaches to conceptions of wisdom and to education.

East/West Conceptions and Manifestations of Wisdom

Wisdom pertains to human affairs (Baltes and Staudinger, 2000; Kramer, 2000); it is ultimately related to human beings' striving for a good life, a life that not only is meaningful and satisfactory to oneself, but also exerts positive influence on others. According to Suh, Diener, Oishi, and Triandis (1998), in Western cultures a good life is attained mostly by doing what a person would like to do; in the East, it is usually doing what a person thinks he or she should do.

It needs to be kept in mind that wisdom is a cultural product that is evaluated, valued, and transmitted by members of societies. Culture provides the framework within which the display, development, and evaluation of wisdom take place (Staudinger, 1996). Members of Eastern and Western cultures have systematic but different conceptions of wisdom, and they often employ their specific conceptions of wisdom in solving everyday problems and judging others (Sternberg, 1985; Yang, 2001). In addition, scholars and theorists also bring their own cultural assumptions with them, which can affect how they conceptualize and study wisdom.

Theorizing Wisdom. Over the past two decades, scholars have proposed many different definitions of wisdom based on research and theory. Although scholars have not reached a consensus on how to define wisdom, most proposed definitions of wisdom could be categorized into four groups.

First, wisdom is defined as a *composite of personality characteristics or competences* (Holliday and Chandler, 1986; Montgomery, Barber, and McKee, 2002; Ardelt, 2003). For example, Ardelt (2003) defines wisdom as a personality characteristic that integrates cognitive, reflective, and affective personality qualities. Second, wisdom is defined as the *positive result of human development* (e.g., Erikson, 1982; Kramer, 2000), either as the end-state of psychosocial development or as capacities that emerge after a higher level of cognitive structure is developed. For instance, Kramer (2000) argues that wisdom is based on relativistic and dialectical reasoning, which takes multiple perspectives into account. Third, Baltes and Kunzmann (2004) define wisdom as *a collective system of knowledge about the meaning and conduct of life*. When wisdom is applied to solve life problems, it brings mind and virtue into perfect orchestration.

Scholars of the fourth group argue that wisdom, the process we can observe in real life, *does not reside only within an individual but emerges from the interaction between individuals and their surroundings*. Even though the original seed of wisdom may reside within an individual, the whole process of wisdom is completed only when the embodiment of wisdom produces certain positive effects for the self and others (Takahashi and Overton, 2005). Moreover, which effects constitute wisdom have to be evaluated not just by the wise individual, but also by other people who sustain the consequences of his or her thoughts and actions (Sternberg, 1998).

What can be inferred from the first three groups of wisdom theories is that many formal theories of wisdom proposed by Western scholars grow from Western conceptions of wisdom. These theorists have focused more on intra-individual or epistemic aspects of wisdom, and may have neglected the contextualized embodiment and resulting effects that might be pivotal to the manifestation and perception of wisdom.

As a result, in my own work as a scholar from the East (Taiwan) who also studied in the West, I have taken a more integrated approach to conceptualizing and conducting research studies in the East. Elsewhere (Yang 2001, 2008a), I have defined wisdom as a positive process that encompasses three core components: (1) *cognitive integration* of what are ordinarily considered separate ideas or conflicting ideals to form a vision promoting the good life, (2) actions that *embody* the integrated thought or vision, and (3) *positive effects* of the actions on the actor and others. In empirical studies, all three core components work together to produce wisdom (Yang, 2008a, 2008b). Wisdom is achieved after a person cognitively makes an unusual integration, embodies his or her ideas through action, and hence brings forth positive effects for both self and others.

Wisdom in the West. Research in the West has tended to arise from the first three conceptions of wisdom discussed above. Sternberg (1985) found that North American conceptions of wisdom consisted of reasoning ability, sagacity, learning from ideas and environment, judgment, expeditious use of information, and perspicacity. Canadian conceptions of wisdom consisted of exceptional understanding of ordinary experience, judgment and communicative skills, general competencies, interpersonal skills, and social unobtrusiveness (Holliday and Chandler, 1986). Hispanic conceptions of wisdom emphasize spirituality (instead of cognition), attitude toward learning (instead of possessing knowledge), and actual acts of serving and caring (instead of giving good advice) (Valdez, 1994).

Bluck and Glück (2004) investigated manifestations of wisdom from an autobiographical perspective in Germany. They found that wisdom is often employed in making life decisions, managing day-to-day lives, and reacting to negative events. It was manifested in three forms: through empathy and support for others; in taking control of one's life while standing by one's values; and by relying on one's knowledge and experience while maintaining flexibility.

In their study of North American adults, Montgomery, Barber, and McKee (2002) found that wisdom was often displayed through guidance, knowledge, experience, moral principles, time, and compassionate relationships. Their nominators were more likely to describe positive influences of wise persons as a form of received guidance from a first-person perspective. For example, when asked to describe a wise person, one participant said, "I was inspired by him to go to college . . . . And I think that was a wise decision, and it was inspired by him" (p. 144).

Wisdom in the East. As discussed earlier, wisdom conceived in the Eastern worldview is thought to function in a similar manner as Tao (Yang and Sternberg, 1997). In Taiwan, a wise person is expected to possess a broad range of competencies and knowledge, to be benevolent and compassionate toward others, to hold profound yet open-minded attitudes about life, and to remain modest and unobtrusive in social interactions (Yang, 2001). Takayama's 2002 study found that many Japanese stress practical and experiential aspects of wisdom rather than abstract thinking. In Japan, wisdom consists of four core dimensions: knowledge and education, understanding and judgment, sociability and interpersonal relationships, and introspective attitudes (Takahashi and Overton, 2005). For Tibetan Buddhist monks, wisdom includes attributes such as recognizing Buddhist truths; realizing emptiness is the true essence of reality; becoming the nonself; existing beyond suffering; being honest and humble; being compassionate to others; respecting others; treating all creatures as worthy and equal; having the ability to distinguish good from evil; and being efficient in projects (Levitt, 1999). Content analyses of the *Bhagavad Gita*, the most influential text of Hindu philosophy and religion, have found that for Hindus wisdom is related more to control over desires, renunciation of materialistic pleasure, emotional regulation, self-contentedness, compassion and sacrifice, insight and humility, yoga, decisiveness, duty and work, love of God, and knowledge of life (Jeste and Vahia, 2008).

A previous study found that Easterners tend to hold a more synthetic view of wisdom, stressing both cognitive and affective dimensions, whereas Westerners tend to emphasize only cognitive dimensions (Takahashi and Bordia, 2000). A comparison of Eastern and Western descriptions of wisdom reveals that Easterners tend to put a stronger emphasis on both action and its effects when discussing wisdom, whereas Western models of wisdom stress the cognitive over the notion of practical application (Yang, 2008b).

New Directions for Adult and Continuing Education • DOI: 10.1002/ace

In my own study of Taiwanese Chinese descriptions of wise people (Yang, 2001), real-life wisdom tended to be manifested through wise persons' handling of daily events, managing one's own life, and contributing to social improvement and progress. Taiwanese Chinese tended to frame their descriptions of wise persons through a third-person perspective, an East Asian tendency also noted by Cohen and Gunz (2002). Description from a first-person perspective was not found in my studies (Yang, 2001, 2008a).

In another study, I asked Taiwanese Chinese respondents who were nominated by others as wise persons questions about the wisest things they had done in life (Yang, 2008b). The results showed that wisdom is more often activated when a person is striving to fulfill his or her vision for the good life. Nominees most often mentioned their (1) striving for common good by helping others and contributing to society, (2) achieving a satisfactory state of life, (3) developing and determining life paths, (4) resolving difficult problems at work, and (5) doing the right thing in the face of adversity. Many wisdom nominees' descriptions, such as devoting themselves to care of terminally ill patients, suggested that wisdom, even for the collectivist, is based more on self-defined vision than socially obligated duty.

Wisdom tends to emerge in at least two real-life contexts. One context is developmental; in this context, wisdom involves life decisions and life management. Wisdom entails knowledge and understanding that allows a person to live the best life. The other context is situational; in this context wisdom arises in everyday situations and takes the form of solving problems or resolving crises. Both kinds of context are needed for the development of wisdom. The wisdom nominees became aware of others' needs because of the difficulties they had encountered earlier in life, yet their wisdom emerged not while they were resolving their own personal problems, but when they vowed to make a difference by helping others who faced similar problems.

Implications for Adult Education

Adult education clearly increases people's knowledge, thus potentially helping them to some degree resolve some important life problems (Merriam, Caffarella, and Baumgartner, 2007). But educators can also emphasize the importance of wisdom and do more to help people discover what is of real value in life for them. There are a number of ways to do this. Adult educators could provide an introduction to theories of wisdom and cultural conceptions of wisdom in courses or workshops. The subject of wisdom can also be included in diverse courses that focus on specific professions, considering how learners might embody integrated insights gained from these courses into real-life situations. Teaching can help learners reflect on the relationship between their learning and their vision of a good life, on how to integrate conflicting ideas, on how to apply integrated insights to real-life situations, and on how to evaluate effects of one's action in order to facilitate the development of wisdom.

Second, the use of techniques such as journal keeping and small-group discussion can help adult learners plan, manage, and review wisdom displayed in their lives. Important life experiences can be analyzed for cognitive and embodied integration of learned lessons and for the influences exerted on one's own life and those of others. Educators can facilitate the development of wisdom by encouraging students to examine their underlying assumptions about wisdom and to clarify their visions of what constitutes a good life.

Third, in thinking about how to work with learners seeking or studying wisdom, educators should first think about their own pursuit and attitudes toward wisdom. Because our understanding of wisdom is often confined to particular cultural contexts where we strive to live a good life, incorporating different cultural perspectives acquired from relevant readings and dialogue with members of different cultures can help us gain a more complete understanding of wisdom. This broader understanding of wisdom in turn extends our view of what is important in life.

Finally, educators can develop their own wisdom by becoming aware of cultural differences between the East and the West. For example, educators should be aware that societal differences can strongly influence the cognition and actions of adult learners, and that modern Asians tend to view the world in holistic terms, whereas modern Western learners tend to see the world in more analytic terms. In classrooms and communities, educators should be conscious that Westerners tend to insist on freedom of individual action, desire individual distinctiveness, prefer egalitarianism and achieved status, and believe that rules governing proper behavior should be universal; whereas East Asian learners tend to prefer collective action, desire to blend harmoniously with a group, accept hierarchy and ascribed status, and favor particularistic approaches that take into account the context and the nature of the relationships involved (Nisbett, 2003). In addition, Western educators should be mindful that they have faith in the rhetoric of argumentation, expect learners to communicate their ideas clearly, and usually assign blame to the speaker for not expressing ideas clearly if there is a miscommunication with the audience; East Asian learners, on the other hand, have the tendency to avoid controversy and debate, to be less vocal listeners, and generally assume it is the hearers' responsibility to understand what is being said.

Eastern and Western cultures represent the actualization of distinct development of the possibilities common to all people. The two can complement and enrich one another in the pursuit of wisdom. By incorporating different cultural perspectives in our teaching and by examining the influences of these perspectives on our actions in practice, educators both East and West can display a blended wisdom that is truly transforming.

References

Ardelt, M. "Empirical Assessment of a Three-Dimensional Wisdom Scale." *Research on Aging,* 2003, *25,* 275–324.

Assmann, A. "Wholesome Knowledge: Concepts of Wisdom in a Historical and Cross-Cultural Perspective." *Life-Span Development and Behavior,* 1994, *12,* 187–224.

Baltes, P., and Kunzmann, U. "The Two Faces of Wisdom: Wisdom as a General Theory of Knowledge and Judgment about Excellence in Mind and Virtue vs. Wisdom as Everyday Realization in People and Products." *Human Development,* 2004, *47,* 290–299.

Baltes, P. B., & Staudinger, U. M. "Wisdom: A Metaheuristic (Pragmatic) to Orchestrate Mind and Virtue Toward Excellence. "*American Psychologist,* 2000, *55,* 122–136.

Bluck, S., & Glück, J."Making Things Better and Learning a Lesson: Experiencing Wisdom across the Lifespan." *Journal of Personality,* 2004, *72,* 543–572.

Chan, W.-T. *Instructions for Practical Living and Other Neo-Confucian Writings by Wang Yang-ming.* Translated, with notes. New York: Columbia University Press, 1963.

Chuang Tzu: Basic Writings. Translated by B. Watson. New York: Columbia University Press, 1964.

Cohen, D., & Gunz, A. "As Seen By the Other . . . Perspectives on the Self in the Memories and Emotional Perceptions of Easterners and Westerners." *Psychological Science,* 2002, *13,* 55–59.

Confucius, K.-T. *The Doctrine of the Mean.* Translated by W.-T. Chan. Princeton, N.J.: Princeton University Press, 1963a.

Confucius, K.-T. *Great Learning.* Translated by W.-T. Chan. Princeton, N.J.: Princeton University Press, 1963b.

Confucius, K.-T. *The Analects.* Translated by D. C. Lao. New York: Penguin Books, 1979.

Cottingham, J., Stoothoff, R., and Murdoch, D. *The Philosophical Writings of Descartes: Vol. 1 & 2.* New York: Cambridge University Press, 1985.

Erikson, E. *The Life Cycle Completed.* New York: Newton, 1982.

Geertz, C. *The Interpretation of Cultures.* New York: Basic Books, 1973.

Holliday, S., and Chandler, M. "Wisdom: Explorations in Adult Competence." In J. Meacham (Ed.), *Contributions to Human Development.* Basel, Switzerland: Karger, 1986.

Jeste, D., and Vahia, I. "Comparison of the Conceptualization of Wisdom in Ancient Indian Literature with Modern Views: Focus on the *Bhagavad Gita.*" *Psychiatry,* 2008, *71*(3), 197–209.

Kaufmann, W., and Baird, F. *Ancient Philosophy.* Englewood Cliffs, N.J.: Prentice-Hall, Inc., 1994.

Kramer, D. "Wisdom as a Classical Source of Human Strength: Conceptualization and Empirical Inquiry." *Journal of Social and Clinical Psychology,* 2000, *19,* 83–101.

Lao Tzu. *Tao Te Ching.* Translated by D. C. Lau. New York: Penguin Books, 1963.

Levitt, H. "The Development of Wisdom: An Analysis of Tibetan Buddhist Experience." *Journal of Humanistic Psychology,* 1999, *39,* 86–105.

Mencius. Translated by D. C. Lau. New York: Penguin Books, 1970.

Merriam, S., Caffarella, R., and Baumgartner, L. *Learning in Adulthood: A Comprehensive Guide.* (2nd ed.) San Francisco: Jossey-Bass, 2007.

Montgomery, A., Barber, C., and McKee, P. "A Phenomenological Study of Wisdom in Later Life." *International Journal of Aging and Human Development,* 2002, *54,* 139–157.

Nisbett, R. *The Geography of Thought.* New York: The Free Press, 2003.

Schirokauer, C. *A Brief History of Chinese Civilization.* New York: Harcourt Brace, 1991.

Staudinger, U. "Wisdom and the Social-Interactive Foundation of the Mind." In P. Baltes and U. Staudinger (eds.), *Interactive Mind.* New York: Cambridge University Press, 1996.

Sternberg, R. "Implicit Theories of Intelligence, Creativity, and Wisdom." *Journal of Personality and Social Psychology*, 1985, *49*, 607–627.

Sternberg, R. "A Balance Theory of Wisdom." *Review of General Psychology*, 1998, *2*, 347–365.

Stevenson, H., and Stigler, J. *The Learning Gap.* New York: Simon and Schuster, 1992.

Suh, E., Diener, E., Oishi, S., and Triandis, H. "The Shifting Basis of Life Satisfaction Judgments Across Cultures: Emotions Versus Norms." *Journal of Personality and Social Psychology,* 1998, *74*, 482–493.

Takahashi, M., and Bordia, P. "The Concept of Wisdom: A Cross-Cultural Comparison." *International Journal of Psychology*, 2000, *35*, 1–9.

Takahashi, M., and Overton, W. "Cultural Foundations of Wisdom: An Integrated Developmental Approach." In R. Sternberg and J. Jordan (eds.), *A Handbook of Wisdom: Psychological Perspectives.* New York: Cambridge University Press, 2005.

Takayama, M. "The Concept of Wisdom and Wise People in Japan." Unpublished doctoral dissertation, Tokyo University, Japan, 2002.

Triandis, H. *Individualism and Collectivism.* Boulder, Co.: Westview Press, 1995.

Valdez, J. "Wisdom: A Hispanic Perspective." (Doctoral Dissertation, Colorado State University, 1993). *Dissertation International Abstract*, 1994, *54*, 6482-B.

Yang, S.-y. "Conceptions of Wisdom among Taiwanese Chinese." *Journal of Cross-Cultural Psychology*, 2001, *32*, 662–680.

Yang, S.-y. "A Process View of Wisdom." *Journal of Adult Development*, 2008a, *15*(2), 62–75.

Yang, S.-y. "Real-Life Contextual Manifestations of Wisdom." *International Journal of Aging and Human Development*, 2008b, *67*(4), 273–303.

Yang, S.-y., and Sternberg, R. J. "Conceptions of Intelligence in Ancient Chinese Philosophy." *Journal of Theoretical and Philosophical Psychology*, 1997, *17*(2), 101–119.

SHIH-YING YANG is an associate professor in the Department of Educational Policy and Administration at National Chi Nan University in Taiwan.

6

This chapter discusses the psychology of the inner life and how music as meditation can tap into unitive states of being that lead to inner wisdom.

The Wisdom of the Inner Life: Meeting Oneself Through Meditation and Music

Abraham Sussman, Mitchell Kossak

Educating adults to tap into the wisdom of their inner life can happen in many contexts: higher education classrooms, workshop and retreat settings, and psychotherapy settings. Adults can also facilitate the development of their inner life through various self-directed learning efforts, by learning from life experience, and through cultivating a spiritual life or meditation practice. As psychotherapists in clinical practice for forty and thirty years, respectively, and as workshop and retreat leaders and educators who regularly draw on arts-based activities, we have both experienced the various ways that adults can tap into their inner wisdom.

We have also been active musicians for the past fifty-seven and fifty years, respectively, and have been initiated often into mysteries of our own nature through the music we have played. A particular musical focus of ours has been improvised music with the intent of generating a sense of calm and inner peace. Through a creative exploration of repetitive melodies and rhythm, we often find ourselves tuning to the very silence that underlies the sound. In our experience this helps free one from the mind-mesh of continuous and random mental activity.

Meditation and improvisational music are distinctly different pathways, but they share some essential features. Both are doorways of self-reflection and provide opportunities for aspects of self-realization that may never be found through the language of concepts and ideas, nor through knowledge of the workings of the outer world. Both pathways invite one into the wisdom of the inner life, the rich world that may open with the closing of one's eyes. Both meditation and music point us toward the transformative experience of inner realization, which is a distinct feature of sacred wisdom in

NEW DIRECTIONS FOR ADULT AND CONTINUING EDUCATION, no. 131, Fall 2011 © 2011 Wiley Periodicals, Inc.
Published online in Wiley Online Library (wileyonlinelibrary.com) • DOI: 10.1002/ace.421

many cultures. Wisdom is defined here as knowledge acquired through direct perceptual experience (Husserl, 1912/1989), or *Sophia,* which is found in those who seek a contemplative life in search of truth (Sternberg, 1998), or what the Buddha taught: wisdom as understanding with our whole being through practice (Mosig, 1989).

This inner experience accesses a level of primal feeling and being, bypassing words and language. This may be the field that thirteenth-century mystic poet Jelaluddin Rumi (1995, p. 36) refers to when he writes: "Out beyond ideas of rightdoing and wrongdoing, there is a field. I'll meet you there. When the soul lies down in that grass, the world is too full to talk about language."

While the psychotherapy we have practiced addresses *interpersonal* wisdom—a deepening awareness of self and self in relation to others—our work as educators has led us to another realm of wisdom that we want to address in this chapter, which may be identified as the *intrapersonal:* how a person experiences the workings of one's own mind and emotions (Clark and Dirkx, 2008), and how one gains insight into the very nature of thinking and feeling, that affects and interconnects adult development and adult learning (Merriam, Caffarella, and Baumgartner, 2007). Apart from the world of human relationships and the external world of matter and things, is the internal world of self-observation and self-reflection, what Gurdjieff (1963, 1973), Ouspensky (1977), and Bennett (1983) call self-witnessing and self-remembering. This inward focusing, this contemplation of our own nature, may be called the inner life. It is a distinct form of adult development, but like many capacities, it is a wisdom path that may best be cultivated through practice.

This wisdom path is also a spiritual path, and while there have been some discussions within adult education about spirituality (English and Tisdell, 2010), there's been little discussion about the cultivation of the inner life through music and meditation as a spiritual practice or as a wisdom path. This chapter provides some background from the traditions of Eastern culture, psychology, and specifically music and meditation practice as pathways into the wisdom of the inner life.

Psychology of the Inner Realm and Unitive Experience

The inner realms of meditation and contemplation have been studied for thousands of years in many Eastern cultures, but in the West, this exploration is a relatively new development. Freud (1905/1960) debunked meditation and Eastern spirituality, assigning it to the domain of misplaced libido. But, on this issue, Freud has been overturned. According to Harvard Science Historian Anne Harrington (2009), two seminal turning points altered the West's receptivity to Eastern meditation. The first was the appearance in the United States in the 1920s of two teachers of Zen meditation who differed from the earlier arcane, superstitious, religious, and secretive presenters of Zen in the West. Both Suzuki (1927) and Senzaki and McCandless (1961) were urbane, modern, educated, and familiar enough with Western society to present Zen in a rational, nonreligious form that was quite accessible to Western minds, and both were very well received.

The second historical turning point can be traced to 1957, when psychoanalyst Erich Fromm organized a conference in Mexico City that brought Zen practitioners and senior psychoanalysts together in dialogue, for the first time. In the fifty-plus years since then, respectful interest in Eastern forms of meditation and spirituality has grown rapidly in the West. The key to the rise of popularity has arguably been de-linking these practices from the religious systems with which they had formerly been associated and understanding them in the context of transpersonal psychology, which studies the transpersonal, self-transcendent, or spiritual aspects of the human experience. Transpersonal interest grew from the work of prior pioneers such as Fromm and included an "understanding, and realization of, unitive, spiritual, and transcendent states of consciousness" (Lajoie and Shapiro, 1992, p. 91).

Psychologist William James (1902/1982), who is considered by many to be the father of transpersonal psychology, was interested in such states of mind, and he described transcendent states as a "unitive experience" sometimes amounting to a felt sense of union with other people, other life forms, objects, surroundings, or the universe itself. For James, the unity felt in spiritual matters and in relationship to the greater world can be thought of as a sense of being undifferentiated from the outside world, or in a Buddhist sense, a feeling of oneness. Tibetan teacher Sogyal Rinpoche (1992) refers to spiritual practice as a unitive felt sense of intimacy with the divine, or an "unfolding vision of wholeness . . . a sense of a living and loving interconnection with humanity" (p. 352).

Transpersonal psychologists are interested in many aspects of human potential, including spiritual self-development, peak experiences, mystical experiences, and various forms of meditation. According to these views of transcendence and intra-connectivity, some meditative states produce a shift in brain activity and a sense of unitive experience. The states found in meditation as evidenced in the research on brain activity have been thought of as related to "the presence of God" and "oneness with the universe" (Newberg, D'Aquili, and Rause, 2001, pp. 115–116).

Transpersonal psychologist John Battista (1996) expands on this concept of unitive experience by including embodied states. Battista's eight-stage model of achieving consciousness offers a hierarchy in which level one involves pure physical interaction, level two involves perception through sensory data, and level three includes affects that function as conscious drives. In the fourth level he states that emotions are embodied. Reflective awareness or cognition is a fifth level of consciousness, and the sixth level is self-awareness, in which cognition can be operated on in the imagination. The seventh level refers to information about self-awareness, or the awareness of being aware, and the eighth level involves the universe as a whole or a transcendent consciousness.

Maslow (1964) also includes embodied awareness in his descriptions of peak experiences. According to Maslow, in this framework one may feel lifted out of oneself, in the flow of things, self-fulfilled, engaged in optimal functioning, and filled with a sense of connectivity to self and the world. Grof (1972) has called these states simply transpersonal experiences, by which he means experiences involving "an expansion or extension of consciousness beyond the usual ego boundaries and the limitations of time and space" (p. 49).

Other examples of this embodied approach come from Eastern practices such as tai chi, yoga, chi kung, and the many other body-centered disciplines that are rooted in becoming present in one's awareness of one's own experience.

Music as Meditation: Reaching the Unitive State

Our personal background in this realm of unitive and embodied states of consciousness involves a lifetime of practice in meditation and many years teaching meditation as a tool for self-development. By meditation, we refer to the simple practice, sometimes called *Vipassana*, of sitting silently with a focused concentration on the rhythmic flow of our own breath. Specifically, we have been drawn to another particular practice, sometimes called *Sufi Sesshin*, which involves alternating meditative periods of silence and inward contemplation with experiences of devotional chanting and movement. *Sufi Sesshin* is a specific application of a more general form called Dances of Universal Peace, founded in the late 1960s by an American Sufi and Zen Master from San Francisco, Samuel Lewis. Lewis also was a student in the 1920s and 1930s of the Zen teacher Senzaki, whom Harrington referred to as introducing Zen to the West. Lewis's Dances of Universal Peace are simple circle dances that involve the chanting of mantra, or sacred sounds, drawn from a wide range of the world's sacred traditions. From years of experience teaching these dances and practicing the *Sufi Sesshin* model, we found that the *entrainment* in chanting and movement contributes significantly to the peaceful quality of subsequent inward concentration and enhances the relaxed calm of the meditation. Entrainment is most often talked about in the scientific literature in reference to resonant fields rhythmically synchronizing together, such as brain waves, circadian rhythms, lunar and solar cycles, breathing, circulation, and rhythms found in the nervous system (Thaut, Kenyon, Schauer, and McIntosh, 1999).

Conversely, the deep tranquility of the meditation practice is a natural foundation for the joy and awakened heart-awareness of the Dance.

As with a deep meditative state, while practicing improvisational music which is part of the *Sufi Sesshin*, the mind quiets down, and one's awareness focuses on feeling the rhythm of the music and an increased awareness of the unfolding of the present moment and the silence within. As the mystic Kahlil Gibran (1998), wrote, "In silence things take form, and we must wait and watch" (p. 8). The Sufi mystic Hazrat Inayat Khan (1991), himself a master musician, reminds us, "The seers, the saints, the sages, the prophets, the masters, they have heard that voice which comes from within by making themselves silent" (p. 23). Through engagement in improvisational music with the specific focus of quieting the mind and generating a sense of inner calm, we note that silence is an important key to the opening of the inner life.

This discovery of the silence in the sound and of the sound in the silence may lead to a realization, which many cultural traditions consider an opening to the sacred. This pathway of inner wisdom involves setting aside the mental focus on language and ideas.

When playing improvisational music in this specific and intended way, we always focus on breath and how breath and rhythm become unified. The focus on breath while playing music in a sacred manner is similar to the focus on breath in meditation practice. In both, when breath and rhythm are synchronized there is a natural sense of embodied presence. By refocusing on the breath and on the body, we may experience an immediacy, an immanence that Buber (1970) calls transcendent in that we transcend the perceived division of self as subject and the world as object.

In *Sufi Sesshin* these elements of sound, breath, and rhythm are inherently present, as they are in *Vipassana* meditation. Being less interested in particular content of mental activity allows one to witness the actual workings of the mind. This shift from content to process leads to self-witnessing, which is what Battista describes in his seventh level as an awareness of being aware.

Many musicians have reported similar states of being aware and experiencing a calmer or unitive state of mind and body. Improvisational musicians often talk about feeling a lost sense of time and space and gaining an entry into a continuous and unbroken flow of heightened sensitivity to each passing moment (Rouget, 1985; Jeddeloh, 2003; Burrows, 2004). In writing about transcendent shifts of consciousness in improvisational music, the writer Ralph Ellison (O'Meally, 2001) calls these moments a movement beyond the rational and bordering onto the mystical. He says that these transcendent moments create a shift in internal states of consciousness, which allows for the transcendence of everyday reality.

Neuroscience and Shifts in Consciousness

Correlates to these experiences have been corroborated through empirical research. For example, Newberg and D'Aquili (2000) have found that when stimuli—such as thoughts and stimulation—are blocked out while playing improvisational music, neural flow slows down. According to these researchers, this slowing down creates a deepening sense of focus and calm and an experience of inner calm through neurological balance and a felt sense of embodied unity. More specifically, Burrows (2004), in his research with improvisational musicians, states that there are moments while playing that could be characterized as "achievement of a higher consciousness" or "state of ecstatic being in the moment which transcends the person's everyday experience of the world" (p. 140).

Further studies also show that engagement in musical activity alters consciousness, including changes in time sense, body image, enhanced imagery, and in the release of beta-endorphins in the brain (Strong, 1998). Strong's research demonstrates that trance states produced through musical activity generate heightened states of awareness, including physiological changes such as deep relaxation and mental and emotional integration.

In laboratory research carried out in conjunction with the University of Munich and the University of Vienna (Goodman and Nauwald, 2003), researchers found dramatic psychological and physiological changes occurring in individuals, including a drop in blood pressure and an increase in pulse while the brain simultaneously released beta-endorphins, the body's own opiate. Concurrently, the electric activity of the brain, as evidenced by EEGs, shifted toward theta waves that occur in deep meditation and deep states of creativity.

In the Buddhist and Hindu traditions, music as meditation has been used for centuries as a vehicle toward transcendent experiences (Paul, 2004). Similarly, in Native American and African traditions, the rituals that involve music have been used as a source of transcendent embodied resonance to divine energies (Chernoff, 1979; Harner, 1980; Hart, 1990; Friedman, 2000). In these traditions, it is specifically believed that the drumbeat is the sound of the Great Spirit, which can lead to an embodied and unitive state or a sense of embodied presence (Drake, 1991). In the Aramaic language, the word for Heaven, *shamaya,* refers to the shimmering vibrations of sacred sound (Douglas-Klotz, 2011).

Similarly, studies of meditation have found that long-term effects include a deepened sense of calmness, increased sense of comfort, heightened awareness of the sensory field, and a shift in the relationship to thoughts, feelings, and experience of self (Cahn and Rael, 2006). Biofeedback studies on those who meditate regularly have demonstrated greater levels of alpha activity connected to lower anxiety levels and feelings of calm and positive affect (Brown, 1970a, 1970b; Hardt and Kamiya, 1978). Research also points to experiencing a greater sense of calm and an increased sense of compassion as a result of regular meditation practice (Kabat-Zinn, 1990; Goleman, 2003).

For example, a study comparing twenty monks (ten with extensive experience, ten with moderate experience) with ten controls prior to and during Zen meditation found that slow alpha states appeared in all groups, but theta activity only appeared in the experienced group. Over time, meditators experienced higher relaxation, mental quietness, and sensation of timeless boundless infinity (Chiesa, 2009).

In a recent study involving students who meditated regularly, the students reported explicitly experiencing a sense of calm, compassion, and acceptance. In addition, the students also felt that their meditation experience helped them become more aware of their "inner chatter" and be less affected by it (McCollum and Gehart, 2010).

In her book *My Stroke of Insight,* brain researcher and stroke survivor Jill Nolte Taylor (2008) addresses this unitive field in terms of the mission of the brain's right hemisphere. As she experienced a breakdown, caused by a stroke, in the fact-finding, linear, logical, detail-oriented, language-based left hemisphere, she reports a euphoric peace, realizing the interdependent harmony of the whole universe, which she claims is the work of the right hemisphere.

From this insight, it can be deduced that the quieting of brain chatter, which occurs in the left hemisphere, can be induced through activities that engage the right hemisphere, such as improvisational music and meditation. Both can lead to the qualities of right brain activity that Dr. Taylor talks so elegantly about, such as euphoric transformative experiences and an unfolding of the present moment. And this may serve as the foundation of the wisdom of the inner life.

Tapping into Inner Wisdom: Recommendations and Conclusions

Through years of engagement in meditation and improvisational music with adult learners in a variety of settings, we have felt the deep immersion in the field that Rumi writes about. We have experienced, through the practice of *Sufi Sesshin* where sessions of improvisational music and devotional chant alternate with sessions of silent meditation throughout a daylong or weekend retreat, a sense of deep calm and tranquility. We have found this helps free one from the mind mesh of continuous and random mental activity, with a shift from content to process leading to a sense of self-witnessing or the awareness of being aware. This insight into the very nature of thinking and feeling is an important stage of adult growth and development, a path to wisdom that can be cultivated and refined through simple engagement and practice.

A useful tool can be simply to follow the breath: count four for each in breath and each out breath. This can be enhanced by a steady drumbeat in the same rhythm or by listening to devotional music that follows a steady and rhythmic beat. Learners can do this on their own, or educators can facilitate this in group settings. Of course, like all forms of practice, intention and focus are essential. However, as one improvisational musician said:

"I prepare by not preparing, and that takes a lot of preparation." One might also consider sitting in silence or taking a walk in nature and listening deeply to the sounds. Of course, the wisdom of the inner life can come from engagement in all kinds of artistic process or forms of meditation, such as reflecting on a piece of artwork, or reflecting deeply on an inspirational poem, or just staring into the eyes of the Beloved.

No matter what, the art of turning inward also takes a good amount of letting go to each breath and each moment, where there is no right or wrong, there is only *being*. And in this being lies the field where true wisdom resides. If you close your eyes, we might just meet there.

References

Battista, J. "Consciousness, Information Theory, and Transpersonal Psychiatry." In J. Battista, B. Scotten, and A. Chinen (eds.), *Textbook of Transpersonal Psychiatry*. New York: Basic Books, 1996.

Bennett, J. G. *Awareness of Others*. Bovington, U.K.: Shantock Press, 1983.

Brown, B. B. "Awareness of EEG-Subjective Activity Relationships Detected Within a Closed Feedback System." *Psychophysiology*, 1970a, 7, 451–464.

Brown, B. B. "Recognition of Aspects of Consciousness Through Association with EEG Alpha Activity Represented by a Light Signal." *Psychophysiology*, 1970b, 6, 442–452.

Buber, M. *I and Thou*. (W. Kaufman, trans.). New York: Simon and Schuster, 1970.

Burrows, J. "Resonances: Exploring Improvisation and Its Implications for Music Education." *Dissertation Abstracts International*, 2004, 66(06) (UMI number 9780494).

Cahn, B., and Rael, P. "Meditation States and Traits: EEG, ERP, and Neuroimaging Studies." *Psychological Bulletin*, 2006, 132(2), 180–211.

Chernoff, J. *African Rhythm and African Sensibility*. Chicago: University of Chicago Press, 1979.

Chiesa, A. "Zen Meditation: An Integration of Current Evidence." *The Journal of Alternative and Complementary Medicine*, 2009, 15(5), 585–592.

Clark, M. C., and Dirkx, J. "The Emotional Self in Adult Learning." In J. Dirkx (ed.), *Adult Learning and the Emotional Self*. New Directions for Adult and Continuing Education, no. 120. San Francisco: Jossey-Bass, 2008.

Douglas-Klotz, N. (2011). *Desert Wisdom: A Nomad's Guide to Life's Big Questions from the Heart of the Native Middle East*. Columbus, Ohio: ARC Books, 2011.

Drake, M. *The Shamanic Drum: A Guide to Sacred Drumming*. Bend, Ore.: Maverick Publications, 1991.

English, L., and Tisdell, E. "Spirituality and Adult Education," In A. Rose, C. Kasworm, and J. Ross-Gordon (eds.), *Handbook of Adult Education*. Thousand Oaks, Calif.: Sage, 2010.

Freud, S. "Three Essays on the Theory of Sexuality." In *Standard Edition*, 7, pp. 123–246. London: Hogarth Press, 1905/1960.

Friedman, R. L. *The Healing Power of the Drum*. Reno, Nev.: White Cliffs Media, 2000.

Gibran, K. *The Beloved: Reflections on the Path of the Heart*. (J. Walbridge, trans.). New York: Penguin, 1998.

Goleman, D. J. *Destructive Emotions: How Can We Overcome Them? A Scientific Dialogue with the Dalai Lama*. New York: Bantam Books, 2003.

Goodman, F., and Nauwald, N. *Ecstatic Trance: New Ritual Body Postures*. Holland: Binkey Kok, 2003.

Grof, S. "Varieties of Transpersonal Experiences: Observations from LSD Psychotherapy." *Journal of Transpersonal Psychology*, 1972, 4(1), 45–80.

Gurdjieff, G. *Meetings with Remarkable Men*. New York: EP Dutton, 1963.

Gurdjieff, G. *Views from the Real World: Talks of G. I. Gurdjieff*. New York: EP Dutton, 1973.

Hardt, J. V., and Kamiya, J. "Anxiety Change Through Electroencepha-Lographic Alpha Feedback Seen Only in High Anxiety Subjects." *Science*, 1978, *201*, 79–81.

Harner, M. *The Way of the Shaman*. San Francisco: Harper & Row, 1980.

Harrington, A. "A History of Compassion in the Lab and Clinic." Presentation at the 2009 *Meditation and Psychotherapy* Conference. Boston, May 2009.

Hart, M. *Drumming at the Edge of Magic*. New York: HarperCollins, 1990.

Husserl, E. *Ideas Pertaining to a Pure Phenomenology and to a Phenomenological Philosophy* (R. Rojcewicz and A. Schuwer, trans.). Norwell, Mass.: Kluwer Academic, 1989. (Original unpublished manuscript 1912.)

James, W. *The Varieties of Religious Experience: A Study in Human Nature*. New York: Random House, 1982. (Original work published 1902.)

Jeddeloh, S. "Chasing Transcendence: Experiencing 'Magic Moments' in Jazz Improvisation." Unpublished doctoral dissertation, Fielding Graduate Institute, 2003. Dissertation Abstracts International (UMI No. 3103587).

Kabat-Zinn, J. *Full Catastrophe Living: Using the Wisdom of Your Body and Mind to Face Stress, Pain, and Illness*. New York: Dell, 1990.

Khan, H. I. *The Mysticism of Sound and Music: The Sufi Teachings of Hazrat Inayat Khan*. Boston: Shambhala, 1991.

Lajoie, D. H., and Shapiro, S. I. "Definitions of Transpersonal Psychology: The First Twenty-Three Years." *Journal of Transpersonal Psychology*, 1992, *24*(1), 79–98.

Maslow, A. *Religious, Values and Peak Experiences*. New York: Viking Press, 1964.

McCollum, E., and Gehart, D. "Using Mindfulness Meditation to Teach Beginning Therapists Therapeutic Presence: A Qualitative Study." *Journal of Marital and Family Therapy*, 2010, *36*(3), 347–360.

Merriam, S., Caffarella, R., and Baumgartner, L. *Learning in Adulthood: A Comprehensive Guide,* (2nd ed.). San Francisco: Jossey-Bass, 2007.

Mosig, Y. D. "Wisdom and Compassion: What the Buddha Taught a Psycho-Poetical Analysis." *Journal of Theoretical and Philosophical Psychology*, 1989, *9*(2), 27–36.

Newberg, A., and D'Aquili, M. D. "The Neuropsychology of Religious and Spiritual Experience." In J. Anderson and R.K.C. Forman (eds.), *Cognitive Maps and Spiritual Maps* (pp. 251–266). Charlottesville, N.C.: Imprint Academic, 2000.

Newberg, A., D'Aquili, E., and Rause, V. *Why God Won't Go Away*. New York: Ballantine, 2001.

O'Meally, R. G. (ed.). *Living with Music: Ralph Ellison's Jazz Writings*. New York: Modern Library, 2001.

Ouspensky, P. D. *In Search of the Miraculous*. New York: Harcourt Brace, 1977.

Paul, R. *The Yoga of Sound: Healing and Enlightenment Through the Sacred Practice of Mantra*. Novata, Calif.: New World Library, 2004.

Rinpoche, S. *The Tibetan Book of Living and Dying*. San Francisco: Harper, 1992.

Rouget, G. *La Musique et la Trance [Music and trance]*. Paris: Gallimard, 1985.

Rumi, J. *The Essential Rumi*. (C. Barks, with J. Moyne, A. J. Arberry, and R. Nicholson, trans.). San Francisco: Harper San Francisco, 1995, p. 36.

Senzaki, N., and McCandless, R. *The Iron Flute*. New York: Charles Tuttle, 1961.

Sternberg, R. "A Balance Theory of Wisdom." *Review of General Psychology*, 1998, *2*(4), 347–365.

Strong, J. (1998). "Rhythmic Entrainment Intervention: A Theoretical Perspective." *Open Ear Journal*, 2. Retrieved May 21, 2011, from http://www.stronginstitute.com/resources/article/8

Suzuki, D. T., *Essays in Zen Buddhism: First Series*. New York: Grove Press, 1927.

Taylor, J. *My Stroke of Insight*. New York: Viking Penguin, 2008.

Thaut, M., Kenyon, G., Schauer, M., and McIntosh, G. "The Connection Between Rhythmicity and Brain Function." *Engineering in Medicine and Biology Magazine*, 1999, *18*(2), 101–108.

ABRAHAM SUSSMAN, PsyD, is a licensed clinical psychologist, a senior teacher of the Sufi Ruhaniat International, and a mentor teacher of and musician for the Dances of Universal Peace.

MITCHELL KOSSAK, PhD, is an assistant professor and a division director of expressive therapies at Lesley University, and a licensed clinical counselor and professional musician.

7

This chapter explores how the spiritual and cultural contexts of wisdom and Black women's knowing and dialogues on race can facilitate cross-cultural and within-group understandings of race, gender, and identity in teaching and learning.

Our Healing Is Next to the Wound: Endarkened Feminisms, Spirituality, and Wisdom for Teaching, Learning, and Research

Chinwe L. Okpalaoka, Cynthia B. Dillard

Wisdom, as defined in this chapter, is not a static concept. It is not some virtue about which one can say that one has finally arrived. Rather, wisdom, like spirituality, both develops and is understood in a cultural context (Tisdell, 2003; Dillard, 2006) and is partly about healing the human spirit; yet, it develops with the experience gained from ongoing dialogue as we are going to demonstrate in this chapter.

This chapter arises from dialogue culled from a yearlong doctoral seminar in which both authors participated. We are both African ascendant women who teach and learn in a higher education setting. Dillard (2006) attributes the notion of ascendancy to Kohain Hahlevi, who coined the term African "ascendant" to imply a progressive movement that calls us to consider a different discourse for the ways we talk about people of African origin. As one of the professors who co-taught the seminar (Cynthia) and a college administrator who was a doctoral student at the time of the seminar (Chinwe), we are going to draw from wisdom that is grounded in Black feminist thought and in endarkened feminist epistemology (Dillard, 2006; Dillard & Okpalaoka, 2011). An *endarkened feminist epistemology* articulates how reality is known when based in the historical roots of global Black feminist thought and when understood within the context of reciprocity and relationship. The notion of reciprocity and relationship is echoed in the works of scholars like Johnson-Bailey and Alfred (2006) and Johnson-Bailey (2010)

New Directions for Adult and Continuing Education, no. 131, Fall 2011 © 2011 Wiley Periodicals, Inc.
Published online in Wiley Online Library (wileyonlinelibrary.com) • DOI: 10.1002/ace.422

whose position on the use of dialogue for transformational teaching and learning also supports the work we have undertaken in this chapter.

We will begin by first explaining the context of the discussions from which the dialogue used in this chapter was selected, and define wisdom as we use it here. Next, because understandings of wisdom continue to develop partly through dialogue, we will offer our dialogue on emerging wisdom. Finally, we will draw some tentative conclusions on what this all means for practice.

The Learning Context of Wisdom

The context of this dialogue on the wisdom of Black women's voices arises from a yearlong doctoral seminar entitled *Spirit, Race, and Dialogue (SRD)*. This course was conceived and co-taught by two faculty (one European American, one African American), guided by their deep (albeit differing) theoretical and cultural commitments to spirituality, endarkened/Black feminisms, antiracism, narrative/qualitative research, and transformative critical pedagogies in teacher education. The course was guided by three core questions that we explored in various ways throughout our year together:

1. Why are we here?
2. Why do so many feel a sense of angst and limit, especially as teachers and researchers who care deeply about social justice and multiculturalism?
3. Is it possible to heal ourselves, our work, our understandings of each other, and our research, particularly around race?

Further, the seminar was designed to be both progressive and cumulative. During fall quarter, we engaged in "The Conversation," where we read, studied, and engaged considerable time and energy developing theoretical understandings of race, spirituality, and dialogue. This was collective time, spent mostly as a large group. Winter quarter, which we titled "Living Ground," was a time for living and experiencing one another through a series of racial/spiritual experiences. We continued to study, write, reflect, and engage, this time in small, cross-racial groups. Spring quarter, called "Witnessing Experience," was used as research space to analyze our experiences of fall and winter quarters, and their connections to our teaching and research lives.

A central commitment of the *SRD* seminar was to explicitly engage theories and texts centered on spirituality and feminisms that might help us unpack our discomfort with race and identity *across* our racial/ethnic differences. However, during spring quarter, we also engaged in necessary conversations and dialogues that were conducted *within* our racial/ethnic groups. In other words, through our actions and pedagogies, the two instructors made explicit the importance of work within European and

African ascendant groups, conversations, and engagements led by the faculty member of the same racial identity group.

This chapter arises from the conversations of the African ascendant women's group, conversations that demonstrate the ways that Black women's wisdom is distinct, useful, and relevant not simply in cross-cultural teaching and learning but for our personal healing and critical affirmation (hooks & West, 1991). We argue here that both are necessary for research, teaching, and learning as sacred work (Dillard & Okpalaoka, 2011). This is the ground from which wisdom, from an endarkened perspective, arises.

When we speak of wisdom, Collins (2000) guides us, arguing that Black women, out of necessity, have relied on a collective set of experiences particular to African American women from which our world view arises. Other scholars in adult education such as Sheared (1994) and Johnson-Bailey (2001) have discussed this as well. Thus, we have had access to a different epistemology by which we assess truth, one that is widely accepted within community. As Black women, an understanding of the distinction between knowledge and wisdom is crucial to our survival: We "cannot afford to be fools of any type, for our objectification as other denies us the protections that White skin, maleness, and wealth confer" (Collins, 2000, p. 257). So wisdom, from an endarkened/Black feminist standpoint, encompasses a set of experiential principles or "lessons" arising from Black women's experiences that, "when shared and passed on, become the collective wisdom of Black women's experiences" (Collins, 2000, p. 256).

The Wisdom of Dialogue

But what do such dialogues look like and reveal? This section focuses on showing the wisdom of endarkened feminist dialogues held by the African ascendant women during the class. While we have constructed this dialogue from pieces of our journals and other documents written during the *SRD* seminar, we hope to demonstrate the ways that the wisdom of endarkened/Black feminism both guided our discussion and opened a way for new Black women's wisdom to arise. As such it continues to create spaces where we can more deeply see the wisdom of Black knowing and the spirituality of Black peoples as informing both the difficult conversations around racism and sexism and their influence on/in our academic lives. These are the key lessons we've learned in dialogues with other Black women around spirit, race, and gender that are important to addressing the angst we often feel across and within our differences. The wisdom we speak about is about healing and connectedness, and facilitating both concepts within oneself and others in our community. While we have intentionally left this wisdom embedded within the narrative, the reader will find what we believe are the most salient lessons—***Black women's wisdom***—highlighted in ***bold italics*** within the following text. Our hope is that this wisdom will provide insights that also help others heal.

New Directions for Adult and Continuing Education • DOI: 10.1002/ace

The particular components of wisdom that emerged during our year-long conversation are incorporated in the dialogue below and have been categorized into the following: the importance of naming; telling healing stories; listening and connecting to spirit; and relating within and beyond the cultural community.

Naming

CYNTHIA: It seems to me that, given the connections and conversations that we have engaged in, that hooks's (1993) notion of being Sisters of the Yam (SOTY) fits us too. We are sisters who are about the business of healing. Naming ourselves also allows us all to have a substantive and personal relationship with the thing named. I feel like we are on the cusp of something bigger than we may even imagine . . . I say that because, as you've suggested, there is very little out there about sisters (or African ascendant people, more broadly) engaged in healing and self-affirmation of who we are the way we are. This is one of those productive spaces . . . But what I am struck by are the limits of the language of research to really accommodate what I experience and hear and see as the *"data"* of our stories.

CHINWE: In your autobiographical poem, "A Literate Life," you speak about not finding stories about you and people like you in assigned texts when you were growing up, and later finding the space in high school debate team to read stuff that sounded like you. And now, as Alice Walker (1983) suggests, *we have the responsibility to create the stories that we should have been able to read [about Black women's lives].*

CYNTHIA: Yes. I talked about that in my autobiography when I said:

> I'm sharing myself/with the rest of the world/I'm writing life now/and reading it too/Through all of these trials and tribulations/I know I've got something to say/It sounds like me/It is me/And people need/to hear my voice/tell my story.

CHINWE: You also speak of our stories as gifts . . . *If we understand that what we are sharing is more than data, that we are giving our stories as gifts to one another, then we will understand that when anyone offers us a glimpse into their pain, dreams, hopes, whatever . . . we should receive it with open hands, gently and honorably, and treasure it for the privilege it is.* Otherwise, as sisters, we risk falling back into silence for the sake of self-preservation. It is a sad state when we are silenced by our oppressors only to find that we are also silenced in the very places we should feel safe.

CYNTHIA: And I am reminded of Audre Lorde's (1984) words about the need for Black people to speak, regardless of the attempts by others to silence us: "I was going to die, if not sooner, then later, whether or not I had ever spoken myself. My silences had not protected me. Your silences will not protect you either" (p. 41). She goes on to say what I believe is the

New Directions for Adult and Continuing Education • DOI: 10.1002/ace

actual work that we might do to respond to being oppressed by others when articulating our realities:

> But for every real word spoken, for every attempt I ever made to speak those truths for which I am still seeking . . . it was the concern and caring of all those women which gave me strength and enabled me to scrutinize the essentials of my living (p. 41).

CHINWE: What happened when we first shared our creative autobiographies was what I had longed for within and without academic circles. Like with most pain and anger, we have focused too much outside of ourselves. This is where victims like to linger. *As long as we can stay in that place of blaming every perpetrator of the sin except ourselves, as long as we can cradle the hurts and pain, even embrace them, then we will never look to say, "What now?"/"What next?"* The challenge we face is in choosing to work through our anger even in the face of the ever-existing structural, social, personal racism. This is risk-taking, *naming* our many circumstances and focusing on ourselves for a change.

Some may read this as absolving the perpetrators of their part in this. Not so. I/We need to ask: How am I contributing to the empowerment of others who continue to shame me and silence me? Because, when I do this, I am telling them: "My self-worth depends on how you make me feel." Cynthia, what you are saying is that *I have the power to be who I was created to be and I am empowered when I realize that.*

CYNTHIA: We have to speak. Speak. And speak some more. Speak until the words feel comfortable in your mouth. *Speak words in ways that have love at the center, especially love of yourself.* And speak them because (and Maya Angelou comes to my mind here) we have the responsibility, once we have learned something or have healed something, to go and teach, to heal someone else. *We "fight the fight" by showing up healthy, strong, whole, with a great sense of what OUR part of the work is, our purpose for being here at this moment on this Earth in these bodies.* These beautiful bodies! Again Audre Lorde's (1984) words are key here:

> My fullest concentration of energy is available to me only when I integrate all the parts of who I am, openly . . . Only then can I bring myself and my energies as a whole to the service of those struggles which I embrace as part of my living (pp. 120–121).

Telling Healing Stories

CHINWE: You also speak of our purpose, and how we heal by showing up. I am reminded of the autobiographical poem "Fully Present" that I wrote for our *SRD* class. In it, I write of the struggle of allowing my authentic self to show up in the academy without fear of rejection of the role that spirit plays in the work that I do. I believe that writing poetry might be a way of telling healing stories. Here's an excerpt from the poem:

> As I get older/As life seasons change/Being my authentic self/Has become very critical/To my spiritual, emotional and/Even physical wellbeing/My twenties and thirties were years of/Morphing into everything/That was required of me/The forties have brought the wisdom/And the urgency of being true to myself . . . /I promised to be true to myself/As I began this decade/Yet, have I been true to myself/In all the many spaces/I am privileged to occupy?

I brought the last question to our SOTY gatherings, a space that welcomed all of me: my spirit, soul, and body. In this space, *I learned that the healing of my whole self was critical to doing race and identity work.* In this space, I came to confront my struggles in the academy as a student who was Black, female, and Christian, and how these identities were fractured in various contexts. In this space, *I embrace all of who I am with the understanding that I need to be fully present in all the contexts I occupy, including the academy.*

Listening and Connecting with Spirit

CYNTHIA: *We have to learn to listen with the body, mind, and spirit and not privilege our minds or personalities, as we have learned to do as "educated" women . . .*

CHINWE: I agree and I ask myself:

> When did the separateness begin for me?/When did I learn that the spiritual/Should be neatly packaged and put as far away/From academe's intellectual minds as possible?/My first encounters in graduate school taught me to/Hide this vital part of my existence/To fit my "new" world/And so I struggled . . . /To wrap my mind, spirit around this fact/That I will now have to live as two persons/Then this invitation came/To dialogue about race and spirit.

What followed was a reclaiming of spirit, as manifested in defining myself as Christian and connecting to Christ as a source of inspiration and wholeness. The *SRD* class provided the context in which I could articulate the fullness of who I was: spirit, soul, and body. For me, *this was wisdom—that I could reclaim and reconnect to spirit and give voice to it in the multiple contexts I occupy.*

CYNTHIA: Chinwe, that is the sort of consciousness that we must consistently and consciously express and live. India Arie's song "I Choose" just popped into my head—we choose our responses to issues that arise around spirit, race, and identity because our healing is in the choices we make. Despite the anger. Despite the pain. Despite our weariness at folks continuing to expect us to always teach [about race, nationality, gender, difference]. Despite the ignorant questions and assumptions about us, bell hooks (1992) says:

> I choose to create in my daily life/Spaces of reconciliation and forgiveness
> Where I let go of past hurt, fear and shame/And hold each other close
> It is only in the act and practice/Of loving Blackness/That we are able
> To reach and embrace the world/Without destructive bitterness
> And ongoing collective rage (p. 1).

CHINWE: When you speak of the weariness that we experience from the emotions caused by ignorance, assumptions, anger, hurt, fear, and shame, you remind me of the emotions that I see as accompanying race talk. I ask myself, "What are the emotions we fear the most that will come up?" Does doing this work in love and with spirit mean an avoidance of emotions?

CYNTHIA: All of which leads us to ask, "How do we respond to that every-day assault on our spirits?" My experiences suggest that part of *our healing is wrapped up in our being honest and focused, in dogged pursuit of our work.* Such response is possible when we are spiritually grounded, both individually as well as in a cultural community. I believe a cohesive world-wide Black collective agenda requires us to also be "individually" strong and healthy within the context of our communities. *It is time to stop telling lies to ourselves about what we coulda/shoulda/woulda done or accomplished if not for (my awful ex, some racist professor, a hurtful interaction with another sister, fill in the blank). This is our life, the real show and not a dress rehearsal.* And as hooks (1993) suggests:

> Solitude is essential to the spiritual for it is there that we can not only com-mune with divine spirits but also to listen to our inner voice . . . without knowing how to be alone, we cannot know how to be with others and sus-tain the necessary autonomy (p. 186).

Relating Within and Beyond a Cultural Community

CHINWE: *If everyone involved in a relationship is in it for the long haul, then it is critical to work through the necessary "mess" and believe that, because of love and spirit, we will be okay on the other side.*

CYNTHIA: The *SRD* course has been very personal talk, where *one must raise questions not just to the other, but maybe more importantly to the self.* These inner spaces have been sometimes painful and difficult spaces to explore. Many of us have described what we've come to call psychic assaults, places where *we have both been disconnected from or distorted through our roots/heritages but also where we ourselves have purposely dis-connected or distorted ourselves in order to survive psychic assaults.* Our SOTY dialogue has helped us to see these distortions as Black women, allowing us to deepen our understanding of our "stuck places," our hurts, our desire for validation and love, our judgments when we don't get what we were expecting (from colleagues, friends, each other). But while our talk has deepened our understanding and empathy, it has also led to new insights that have uncovered more stuck places, present before but beyond our awareness.

CHINWE: *It is difficult for race talk to happen without building relationships first.* If I build a relationship with you, then I can begin to know you and what I know about you will help to filter what I hear you say, even within the painful and difficult spaces. When you speak about more stuck places you appear to be saying that this race work and race talk is continuous and ongoing?

CYNTHIA: Yes. Appiah (1992) talks about the need to understand and know another deeply and culturally as a prerequisite to productively reading (and thus being with) another. In this case, wisdom is *being grounded in our own cultural realities* as Sisters of the Yam. This is still a difficulty for many, as *we come to race talk differently, with varying ways that we have experienced race and racism and the ways that culture and race work in the world (historically, structurally, spiritually).* There's the need to listen deeply, and it's difficult to balance those differences with talk about/through race, as it raises imbalance in positioning, as we've known it. Who is center? Who is marginalized?

CHINWE: The question of who is marginalized and who is center came up when our conversations turned to the issue of class and how it appears that people who experience class discrimination feel silenced in discussions around race. They are typically accused of trying to equate racism with classism. This may be true for individuals who approach these discussions from a place of refusing to hear the other before they suggest that their pain is like everyone else's. But it is also true that there are African ascendant people who have closed their ears and hearts to the experiences of others, not recognizing that *in talking about race and racism, we need to graciously welcome all the different experiences that participants bring to the discussion.* Their frustration—and ours—lies in the space where bringing up experiences with classism too often steers the conversation away from the truth about race without looking at race and class relationally.

CYNTHIA: Several of the SOTY have expressed frustration with having experienced race and racism as African ascendant women. I call it the weight of Black experience. What do we do with it? Does it raise questions of the possible limits of race talk, particularly across race?

CHINWE: Which is why you continue to bring us back to the notion of healing?

CYNTHIA: Yes. Healing for something bigger than ourselves seems a sort of *liberatory healing,* of sitting down the heaviness of the weight of experience. *I heal myself so that others can heal. I recognize my being as a Black woman in the past, present, and future as a transcendent identity that moves through and beyond the limits of race and gender.*

CHINWE: I am reminded of a documentary, *Color of Fear,* in which a group of men of various ethnic and racial backgrounds model what it means to work through the messiness of race talk. I remember that there was a freedom of expression. There was anger, but in the end there was love. I witnessed men walking through work that was definitely messy. I witnessed their struggles with the reality of how we are all affected by racism. But I saw them help each other work through this process and, yes, they went from using the general "you" and "they" to seeing each other as individuals on the same journey, some further along than others.

CYNTHIA: Our focus on love generally and loving Blackness particularly is the counternarrative. Like hooks (2000) suggests, such love includes empathy, respect, forgiveness, compassion, honesty, trust, sincerity, joy, etc. Most importantly, it is a move away from fear, from holding back and instead towards an embrace of the emotionality and vulnerability of our unknowns. But *love, if it's really unconditional, will carry us through.* We will have to help each other through the process. But, as you have said somewhere else, if done in love and with commitment, "we'll be okay on the other side."

Suggestions for Practice

The key characteristics of wisdom we have highlighted here can be applied to the work we do with all students, but especially adult learners. First, we can teach students to see wisdom in the importance of naming their reality. Only in doing that can teacher and learner begin the healing process that is critical particularly to race work. Wisdom is also the recognition that we must bring our whole selves—spirit, mind, and body—into the multiple contexts we occupy. Adult learners should be encouraged to show up as whole beings in whatever contexts they find themselves. Finally, we must learn to honor the wisdom inherent in all the experiences that learners bring to the classroom. Only then can we begin to achieve the relationship-building that is a necessity for critical conversations.

References

Appiah, A. *In My Father's House: Africa in the Philosophy of Culture.* New York: Oxford University Press, 1992.

Collins, P. H. *Black Feminist Thought: Knowledge, Consciousness, and the Politics of Empowerment.* (2nd ed.) New York: Routledge, 2000.

Dillard, C. B. *On Spiritual Strivings: Transforming an African American Woman's Academic Life.* Albany: State University of New York, 2006.

Dillard, C. B., and Okpalaoka, C. L. "The Sacred and Spiritual Nature of Endarkened Transnational Feminist Praxis in Qualitative Research." In N. K. Denzin and Y. S. Lincoln (eds.), *The Sage Handbook of Qualitative Research.* (4th ed.) Los Angeles: Sage, 2011.

hooks, b. *Black Looks: Race and Representation*. Boston: South End Press, 1992.
hooks, b. *Sisters of the Yam: Black Women and Self-Recovery*. Boston: South End Press, 1993.
hooks, b. *All About Love: New Visions*. New York: William Morrow and Company, 2000.
hooks, b., and West, C. *Breaking Bread: Insurgent Black Intellectual Life*. Boston: South End Press, 1991.
Johnson-Bailey, J. *Sistahs in College: Making a Way Out of No Way*. Malabar, Fla.: Krieger Press, 2001.
Johnson-Bailey, J. "Learning in the Dimension of Otherness: A Tool for Insight and Empowerment." In M. Rossiter and M. C. Clark (eds.), *Narrative Perspectives on Adult Education*. New Directions for Adult and Continuing Education, no. 126. San Francisco: Jossey-Bass, 2010.
Johnson-Bailey, J., and Alfred, M. "Transformational Teaching and the Practices of Black Women Adult Educators." In E. W. Taylor (ed.), *Teaching for Change: Fostering Transformative Learning in the Classroom*. New Directions for Adult and Continuing Education, no. 109. San Francisco: Jossey-Bass, 2006.
Lorde, A. *Sister Outsider*. Freedom, Calif.: The Crossing Press, 1984.
Sheared, V. "Giving Voice: An Inclusive Model of Instruction—A Womanist Perspective." In E. Hayes and S.A.J. Colin (eds.), *Confronting Racism and Sexism*. New Directions for Adult and Continuing Education, no. 61. San Francisco: Jossey-Bass, 1994.
Tisdell, E. J. *Exploring Spirituality and Culture in Adult and Higher Education*. San Francisco: Jossey-Bass, 2003.
Walker, A. *In Search of Our Mother's Gardens: Womanist Prose*. San Diego: Harcourt Brace Jovanovich, 1983.

CHINWE L. OKPALAOKA *is the director of diversity services in the College of Arts and Sciences at The Ohio State University.*

CYNTHIA B. DILLARD *is a professor of multicultural teacher education in the School of Teaching and Learning at The Ohio State University.*

New Directions for Adult and Continuing Education • DOI: 10.1002/ace

8

This chapter offers insights into mentoring men toward wisdom and is based on the notion that growth into a more grounded and connected wisdom entails transformation of the pillars of traditional masculinity: procreating, providing, and protecting.

Mentoring Men for Wisdom: Transforming the Pillars of Manhood

Laurent A. Parks Daloz

"So, what do you advise, Malawi or New Guinea?"

He just looked at me. A long time. A soft smile curled his lips, in his eyes a hint of irony. Not a word.

I had stopped by Adam's office because I was torn between the right thing to do—a job in the planning office of a United Nations agency gathering statistics for Malawi's future educational development—or the challenging thing: two years working with teacher education doing God-only-knew-what in a country barely out of the stone age. I glanced down at the notes on my lap. I had carefully laid out the pros and cons. A previous stint with the Peace Corps in Nepal should have taken care of the adventure thing; wasn't it time now to get serious, do my doctoral studies in work that would position me for career advancement? I looked back up.

The gleam was still in his eyes, his smile still warm. He spoke not a word, but I knew exactly what he had said. I gathered my notes, stood up, shook his hand, thanked him, and headed for New Guinea.

Three years earlier in the same office, Adam had told me I needed more experience before I would be admitted to the doctoral program that he headed, and handed me the name of a school superintendent in West Virginia. "Here," he said, "I'll give him a call. He could use someone like you." That had gone well, and, properly ripened, I had returned to take up my course work and then to receive Adam's blessing to do my fieldwork in New Guinea.

Shortly after I graduated, Adam left his tenured position to return to his native England and move into a second career as an internationally respected mediator, working in the tormented thickets of Biafra, Northern Ireland, and Sri Lanka. But we stayed in touch over the years and I would write long letters

NEW DIRECTIONS FOR ADULT AND CONTINUING EDUCATION, no. 131, Fall 2011 © 2011 Wiley Periodicals, Inc.
Published online in Wiley Online Library (wileyonlinelibrary.com) • DOI: 10.1002/ace.423

detailing my considerably lesser torments, wondering periodically about the meaning and value of it all. He would write back, occasionally confronting, sometimes advising, but always coming alongside and expressing his own wonder at how things are in this life. One late winter afternoon years later, I interviewed him for a book about lives committed to the common good. We met in a nearly empty Cambridge restaurant over coffee. It had grown dark, I recall, and quiet.

We spoke of our respect for the Quaker tradition of peacemaking, and I asked him about the wrenching suffering he had portrayed so graphically in a volume of poetry written out of his experience in Biafra.

"How do you do it?" I asked. "How do you keep from being sucked into that anger and pain—from just giving up in despair?"

His hands circled the now empty mug in a long silence.

"Well," he said finally, "I try to stay detached . . ." He paused again. "But it's not exactly that either. You have to remain connected at the same time. You cannot seal yourself off. If you lose your compassion, you lose everything."

"But how do you do that?" I asked. "How do you hold detachment and compassion together at once?"

"While I was in Sri Lanka," he replied, "I heard the story of Indra's net. The ultimate reality of the universe is a great web in which everything is interconnected, and at each node is a jewel of indescribable beauty. Each node is a living being, and everything is influenced by everything else. You touch any point on the net and the whole net shimmers."

It was as if he had reached into some secret pocket that cold day and placed in my palm a precious stone. It rests now in some hidden fold of my knowing. Far too often I forget it is there, but now and again, groping for something else, I encounter it and I remember. Adam is gone now, but the jewel, his gift, remains.

I have long considered Adam one of the wise men in my life, but he didn't "have" wisdom, he *embodied* it and transmitted it in a thousand ways to countless of us whose lives touched his. I resist defining "wisdom" in the abstract, hovering in the Platonic ethers. It dies there without warmth or a pulse to give it life. To mean anything at all, wisdom must be embodied, must be made real in words and deeds. Wisdom can only come to life in relationship, out of the connections among human beings, each of whom will give it a unique meaning shaped by his or her own human contexts (Buber, 1958).

As a developmentalist, I consider wisdom the highest fulfillment of the potential in all human beings. It is a worthy, even essential, goal, but the degree to which it takes form in us depends on the experiences life sends, and its cultivation demands relentless discernment. We are neither born with it nor assured of its realization. The maturation of wisdom takes time—and experience, sometimes joyful, often harsh. People who speak of a wise child are speaking of innocence, perhaps, or even fresh insight, but not wisdom, not the earned wisdom that comes of the struggled healing of a heart broken, a trust betrayed, a dream shattered.

Moreover, it often appears in imperfect vessels. Few of us are wise in all ways. Rather, we have wise moments, insights, or actions. And like a great wine, though it may be drinkable as it develops, in its finest and fullest manifestation, wisdom requires age, ripening, maturity. It is a kind of meta-knowing, seamlessly integrating tactile, intellectual, emotional, and spiritual understanding. Still, some of us are wiser more often than others, and among the wise we might recognize such characteristics as self-understanding, empathy, compassion, humor, broadmindedness, and complex systemic thought (Kegan, 1998). Notice that in his answer to my question about detachment and compassion, moreover, Adam was holding paradox and thinking dialectically (Rybash, Hoyer, and Roodin, 1986); in the image of Indra's net, he recognized the radical interdependence of life (Daloz, 2004); in the life he lived, he manifested deep humility and fierce commitment. We have described these and other characteristics of mature development in detail in *Common Fire*, our study of people committed to the common good (Daloz and others, 1998).

I treasured my friendship with Adam years before I had a name for it. But it is clear that he was a mentor. Like Virgil leading Dante on his great journey, Adam led the way for me, serving as adviser in Pakistan as I would in New Guinea. As mentors do, he saw me as having something to offer, he set me on my path, and he alternately challenged and supported me along the way, remaining faithful as teacher and friend. Over time, though we often went years without meeting, we shared books and articles we had written and spoke through correspondence of things nearer our hearts. From him I learned such wisdom as I could recognize, and onto him I projected such wisdom as I could imagine. Even now, at tender moments, I find myself asking, "How would Adam hold this?"

The Meaning of Mentoring

Recall that the original Mentor, an old man, was a manifestation of Athena, goddess of wisdom. Thus, Mentor was both god and human, female and male. The embodiment of wisdom, Mentor's highest art is to cultivate wisdom in the protégé through artful dialogue. Sharon Parks and I have identified a number of mentoring functions that occur individually or in communities. Chief among them are *Recognition, Challenge, Support, Inspiration,* and *Presence.* That is, a defining moment in a mentoring relationship occurs when the protégé feels *seen* by the mentor. In some way, we feel pulled out from the crowd; we feel special, acknowledged in a way that we have longed for but rarely known. This is the beginning of self-insight and perhaps of transformation. As the relationship ripens, a complex dance of *challenge* and *support* follows. Skillful mentoring holds these well in balance so that there is neither so much challenge in the absence of support that the protégé loses confidence nor so much support without challenge that no growth occurs. At the same time, the relationship must have direction, purpose, *moral* fire. The art of the mentoring community is to tend that fire, damping it where it flares out of control, fanning it when it burns low. And throughout, the mentor must be *present* for the protégé during their journey together, must remain accountable, respond appropriately in the dance, be a willing foil on whom protégés can project their aspirations (often regardless of whether the mentor feels worthy), and finally offer a blessing as the protégé moves out into the world (Daloz, 1999; Parks, 2000).

Mentoring is ultimately about cultivating a fruitful relationship, one that includes actions as well as words. This may begin between mentor and student, but must expand to include books and media, other students and authorities, and praxis with the world at large. At the same time, the dialogue must also turn inward. It must bring disparate parts of ourselves together. The mentor's job is to help us to connect the dots at ever deeper levels and across ever wider horizons.

Rethinking Masculinity

As I write, *Newsweek*'s cover declares that "The traditional male is an endangered species. It's time to rethink masculinity" (Romano, 2010). This is hardly new. Manhood has been declared in danger any number of times, most recently with the rise of the modern feminist movement four decades ago. Many men did change. But then they were responding to women's changes. This time is different. This time not only have women changed; the world has changed, too.

Traditionally, to be considered successful a man had to do three things well: procreate, provide, and protect. In fact, anthropologists tell us that these have been pillars of manhood in virtually every culture for millennia: we are expected to *procreate* offspring, the more fruitfully the better; *provide* for our family and tribe, the more lavishly the better; and *protect* them, the more fiercely the better (Gilmore, 1990). But in an increasingly urban world, it no longer makes sense for a man to sire as many children as he can; in a society where a single income has lost its potency and women share the workplace, few men can be the sole provider; and in a world of terrorism and roadside bombs, protection is rarely about just being tougher. Among numerous recent articles on the topic, one simply declared "the end of men" (Rosin, 2010). The three pillars of manhood that for eons have framed men's roles and sustained their sense of worth are crumbling. How do we who entered adulthood at an earlier time mentor men toward wisdom for a changed world? Before we address that question, we need to understand more about the particular dynamics of male formation.

Understanding Men's Development. Much has been written about the social construction of masculinities (Brod, 1987; Kilmartin, 2007). More recently, brain research has added significantly to our knowledge of intrinsic differences between the sexes (Sax, 2007). While acknowledging the importance of both nurture and nature, I want to point to a third set of insights from a psychological perspective regarding the formation of masculinity.

Paradoxically, though perhaps not surprisingly, the most profound of these insights came some years ago from women informed by object relations theory, and their insights are still relevant today. Dorothy Dinnerstein (1976) first suggested that the inequities and struggles between the sexes are grounded in the simple but inescapable fact that mothers are women. ". . . [F]or virtually every human," she wrote, "the central infant-parent relationship, in which we form our earliest intense and wordless feelings toward existence, is a relation with a woman" (p. 33). The effect of this reality is very different on boy toddlers, who must at some point *separate from* their mothers, than from girls, who come to identify and thus *connect with* their mothers. This insight was subsequently deepened by Chodorow (1978) and elaborated by Gilligan (1982).

This need to separate from Mother in order to be a real man is rooted in the male soul from the earliest years, as boys learn they will not grow up to be like Mama. The discovery that we are fundamentally *different from* the source of our nourishment comes as a profound shock to a tender three-year-old just discovering that he is a boy. It's not just the "male ego" that's fragile; the very sense of *self* is fragile. Writing about women's psychology, Miller (1976) noted almost in passing that

> . . . men are strongly pulled toward other people sexually and in a more total emotional sense but *they have also erected strong barriers against this pull* [emphasis added]. And here, I think, is the greatest source of male fear: that the pull will reduce them to some undifferentiated mass or state ruled by weakness, emotional attachment, and/or passion and that they will thereby lose the long-sought and fought-for status of manhood (p. 23).

Male Archetypes and Mentors. Since then, many studies of boys have confirmed this work, emphasizing the vulnerability of boys as they struggle to grow a secure sense of self, both in relation to and distinct from their mothers (Kindlon and Thompson, 1999). Happily, a handful have noticed the vital importance of a loving and connected father (or other male) to catch the son as he makes the passage from the realm of women to the realm of men (Snarey and Vaillant, 1993). This is, of course, a primary purpose of the initiation rituals that have served as a sacrament for much of the life of our species. But for many boys today, these rites have dwindled to a driver's license, getting smashed, joining a gang, or having bad sex in the back seat. Moreover, too many fathers are missing from their sons' lives. More than 40 percent of all males today are raised in homes without a resident father (Salzman, Matathia, and O'Reilly, 2005). Indeed, across my thirty-five years of work with men, it is clear that a torn or missing relationship with the father touches deep pain, often acknowledged only years later. Despite heroic efforts by mothers to compensate, many boys suffer what could be called a "connectivity deficit," in that they spend much of their boyhood and subsequent manhood attempting to overcome by justifying their separateness, especially from the feminine. William Pollack (1998) describes the "boy code" that most boys learn: to be stoic, independent, and willing to take risks, and to appear in charge, regardless of what he actually feels. And above all, he must *never* show weakness, cry, or run away. The price for failure is to be called a sissy or, worse, a girl, as if either were something bad. And in a truly jarring cross-cultural study of misogyny, anthropologist David Gilmore (2001) echoes Miller, locating men's pervasive ambivalence toward women in their deep fear "of collapsing ego boundaries . . . and *a return to nothingness* [emphasis added]" (p. 141).

Men's response to this threat of psychic annihilation is fight or flight, and it shows up in the form of two preeminent heroic archetypes: the armored man and the eternal boy. While each represents one end of a spectrum, I have found that elements of each show up in most men.

The armored man fights, sealing himself off from the pain of connection by a range of distancing strategies: machismo, patriarchal claims, hyperrationality, pugnacity, stony silence. Wisdom for him means being tougher and smarter than your enemy. The eternal boy, on the other hand, takes flight. He makes a virtue of his innocence and transparency, valuing his creativity, independence, and freedom from commitments. Like Peter Pan, he fears growing old, loves the light and spirituality, and is repelled by darkness, weight, or "mere" earthly matters. Wisdom he confuses with innocence. Depth psychology knows him as the *Puer Aeternus* (von Franz, 1981).

These heroic images often shape boys' imaginations: the invulnerable flying Superman, the ramblin' steel-jawed gunfighter, the grail-seeking knight. Combining idealism with toughness, they channel male energy and clear a space in the soul for a larger sense of purpose and such critical adult values as honor, integrity, generosity, and willingness to sacrifice (Gurian, 2009). Yet both are immature forms of masculinity, reaction formations born of our early losses; we come by them honestly. Note, for instance, that few of these heroes are at ease with women. After all, the coveted "hero's journey" (Campbell, 1949) begins with departure from the feminine realm of home.

During their twenties and thirties men are building outer strength, testing themselves, finding their place, seeking a mate. They tend to value challenge, competition, fairness, achievement, pushing the limits. Testosterone-driven, many are drawn to exploration and adventure, challenges they hope will make them strong and give them an edge. Psychologist James Hollis (2005) refers to all this as the "first adulthood." The "second adulthood" is about what happens when that world is no longer enough, when failure, betrayal, and the inevitable compromises and losses of midlife arrive. The time of growing up and out is waning; now is the opportunity to grow down and in, to

New Directions for Adult and Continuing Education • DOI: 10.1002/ace

begin to heal our brokenness. It may be a time of confusion, fear, even despair, but it is also a time of radical possibility, a chance to explore the shadow.

Mentoring Men Toward Wisdom

But this will take a new kind of courage, for the journey toward wisdom finally leads homeward. In the end, the hero returns with a gift to his community: his outer armor has become inner strength, his vision is grounded, and he reconnects in solid ways with his people. To do this requires that he acknowledge to himself as well as others his humanity, his vulnerability, his interdependence with others. This can be a tough lift, since to do so is to challenge the very foundation of the autonomous masculinity he has spent so much of his life building.

As I've suggested, one of the early costs of masculine formation is that men split off as "feminine" the gift of connected care from their mothers, which so few received from their fathers. At its heart is the capacity for empathy. Boys are born with this as fully as girls, but often feel forced to cash it in for the benefits of boyhood. The new courage requires men to face down the culture's scorn and relearn mature male care (Noddings, 1984).

Empathy and Engagement. A key finding in *Common Fire* (Daloz and others, 1998) was that at some point during their formative years, almost all our interviewees had experienced what we came to call "a constructive engagement with otherness." That is, by empathizing in a deep way with someone previously viewed as "other," they came to include within their circle those who had been excluded. Experienced mentors instinctively know this—that a key part of their work is to expose their students to differing points of view. Seeing the world through the eyes of the "other" is central to the development of critical and connective thought. "I never feel I understand another person," said a colleague, "until I know *how they are right.*" He then insists that his students incorporate that voice into their own inner dialogue, thus pressing toward a more nuanced and powerful synthesis. Always the differentiation is in the service of a deeper connection.

Engagement with otherness, however, is most powerful when it includes empathy with the pain of the other. Shared suffering connects. This has been dramatically confirmed in recent years through the discovery of "mirror neurons," the receptors in the brain that enable us literally to feel the pain of the other. While both men and women have them, men tend to shut them off much faster, attempting instead to "fix" the trouble (Brizendine, 2010, pp. 96–99). Having systematically staunched their own pain, sitting with the pain of others can be difficult for many men. "Just man up and get on with it!" our culture tells men. Yet while armor protects, it also confines. Letting go of the armor can be frightening—and liberating. "Once you hit your deep grief, once you get way down there," said one man, "you can't fall any further.

You're there." Giving men permission to encounter their grief, and encouraging them to name their pain, is a powerful way that mentors can enhance men's cultivation of wisdom because it dissolves both the armor and the narcissism. Men can start by sitting alone with sad music, watching romantic movies (or for some men violent ones with wrenching outcomes), or reading insightful books about people's inner lives; later they might move to deep journaling. But ultimately, sharing their stories of loss—often around fathers and sons—offers a path into a new way of being and knowing.

Acting for the Common Good. Still, boys fidget, men act. Men need to integrate what they are learning, and many best do it through action. Mentors can foster this integration by challenging men to put their learning to practical use and inspiring them to do so in ways that serve the larger good. In the end, mentoring men for wisdom is about kindling the fire of moral action. Sadly, many young men seem to have missed or lost that fire, turned cynical, or squandered it in self-destructive or callous ways (Kimmel, 2008). Great mentors won't stand for that. They ask big questions and demand worthy dreams (Parks, 2000): *What is your life about? Who are you responsible for? What really matters?* They pass on the fire, they remind their protégés that they matter, they conjure courage to move into the world and make a difference.

Conclusion

As we work to reimagine the three pillars of manhood, let's recognize that there is both gain and loss in early male formation: men gain a certain clarity, power, and even vision in their separateness, yet may pay the cost in mutuality, responsiveness, and connectedness. Mentors can help men heal their connectivity deficit while retaining the strengths of their distinctiveness by reminding them that they have within themselves what they need for the journey and that some men are already underway. As men engage more fully in the direct care of children or the larger community, they may expand the meaning of *procreation* to include helping to build a more caring and vibrant society. As they recognize their intrinsic interdependence, they may recast *providing* to include what many traditional cultures have always known: that generosity is the highest mark of a virtuous man (Gilmore, 1990). And as they more deeply acknowledge their own vulnerability and strengthen their capacity for empathy, they may recognize that *protection* must include the courageous quest for alternatives to violence.

Finally, as we do the inward work of discovering our interdependence, of knowing our fellow humans as we are known, and of transforming what it means to be men at this time in history, we add a fourth pillar, *partnership*: a partnership with women that is neither oppressive nor deferential, a partnership with all people that is neither condescending nor obsequious, a partnership with all life on the planet that is finally reverential.

The challenges of this century are daunting. Real men have always responded to the call of the heroic journey: to challenge, to justice, to compassion, and finally to wisdom. Our partnership with one another in the quest to transform the male story has just begun.

References

Brizendine, L. *The Male Brain*. London: Bantam, 2010.

Brod, H. (ed.). *The Making of Masculinities*. Boston: Allen & Unwin, 1987.

Buber, M. *I and Thou*. New York: Scribners, 1958.

Campbell, J. *The Hero with a Thousand Faces*. Princeton N.J.: Princeton University Press, 1949.

Chodorow, N. *The Reproduction of Mothering*. Berkeley: University of California Press, 1978.

Daloz, L. *Mentor*. San Francisco: Jossey-Bass, 1999.

Daloz, L. "Transformative Learning for Bioregional Citizenship." In E. O'Sullivan, and M. Taylor (eds.), *Learning Toward Ecological Consciousness*. New York: Palgrave, 2004.

Daloz, L., Keen, C., Keen, J., and Parks, S. *Common Fire*. Boston: Beacon, 1998.

Dinnerstein, D. *The Mermaid and the Minotaur*. New York: Harper & Row, 1976.

Gilligan, C. *In a Different Voice*. Cambridge, Mass.: Harvard University Press, 1982.

Gilmore, D. *Manhood in the Making*. New Haven, Conn.: Yale University Press, 1990.

Gilmore, D. *Misogyny: The Male Malady*. Philadelphia: University of Pennsylvania Press, 2001.

Gurian, M. *The Purpose of Boys*. San Francisco: Jossey-Bass, 2009.

Hollis, J. *Finding Meaning in the Second Half of Life*. New York: Gotham, 2005.

Kegan, R. *In Over Our Heads*. Cambridge, Mass.: Harvard University Press, 1998.

Kilmartin, C. *The Masculine Self*. New York: Sloan, 2007.

Kimmel, M. *Guyland: The Perilous World Where Boys Become Men*. New York: HarperCollins, 2008.

Kindlon, D., and Thompson, M. *Raising Cain*. London: Penguin, 1999.

Miller, J. *Toward a New Psychology of Women*. Boston: Beacon, 1976.

Noddings, N. *Caring*. Berkeley: University of California Press, 1984.

Parks, S. *Big Questions, Worthy Dreams*. San Francisco: Jossey-Bass, 2000.

Pollack, W. *Real Boys*. New York: Holt, 1998.

Romano, A. "Men's Lib." *Newsweek*, Sep. 27, 2010, pp. 43–49.

Rosin, H. "The End of Men." *The Atlantic*, Jul./Aug., 2010. Retrieved May 4, 2011, from www.theatlantic.com/magazine/archive/2010/07/the-end-of-men/8135/2/

Rybash, J., Hoyer, W., and Roodin, P. *Adult Cognition and Aging*. Oxford, U.K.: Pergamon, 1986.

Salzman, M., Matathia, I., and O'Reilly, A. *The Future of Men*. New York: Palgrave Macmillan, 2005.

Sax, L. *Boys Adrift*. New York: Basic Books, 2007.

Snarey, J., and Vaillant, G. *How Fathers Care for the Next Generation*. Cambridge, Mass.: Harvard University Press, 1993.

von Franz, M. *Puer Aeternus*. Boston: Sigo Press, 1981.

LAURENT A. PARKS DALOZ *is a senior fellow at the Whidbey Institute in Clinton, Washington. A former professor in adult education at Lesley College, he has taught at the Harvard Graduate School of Education and Columbia Teachers College.*

9

This chapter reflects on the human quest to understand both the "why" and the "how" of existence itself and suggests that while we can be taught about wisdom, we can only learn to be wise.

Teaching, Learning, and the Human Quest: Wisdom

Peter Jarvis

Why is there a universe?
Why do we exist?
How can I best live in this mysterious—and yet commonplace—everyday world?

Unanswerable questions—but ones that humankind has asked since time immemorial; wise people, and those who are not so wise, have grappled with or provided their answers to them. This is where wisdom finds its place. As the chapters in this volume show, wisdom is a complex phenomenon: it finds its home primarily but not exclusively in theology, philosophy, psychology, education—that is, in the humanities—and in life itself. In a paradoxical manner, wisdom finds its home in the world of the unanswerable, where there are no empirical proofs and no obvious answers. Wisdom actually finds its place when we consider the mystery of our being and the inevitability of our becoming, when we think of the universe and life itself and realize that we will probably never know why either should be; but the fact that we have no answers does not mean that we can stop asking the questions, for this would deny the nature of our humanity (Pasternak, 2007; Jarvis, 2009).

This is also where I began my academic career—teaching religious studies from a sociological perspective and ethics or moral philosophy. Indeed, we can learn the historical and the contemporary answers to this human quest, but that does not necessarily make us wise; having knowledge of wisdom is not being wise. We can educate, but formation and mentoring (Daloz, this volume) might be better concepts when we think about preparing people to grow wise. Or we may just grow wise by having the experiences of learning in and from our lives. One of the inevitable outcomes of

NEW DIRECTIONS FOR ADULT AND CONTINUING EDUCATION, no. 131, Fall 2011 © 2011 Wiley Periodicals, Inc.
Published online in Wiley Online Library (wileyonlinelibrary.com) • DOI: 10.1002/ace.424

seeking to understand experiential learning is recognizing that we learn more than we consciously know, for this is about tacit knowledge (Polanyi, 1967), and wisdom finds its place here.

As a lecturer of religious studies earlier in my career, I had reached the conclusion that all theologies are responses to the questions "why?" and so it is not surprising that from the outset of my studies of human learning, I have been concerned with what I then called, and still call, *disjuncture*, which is the feeling of no longer feeling at home in the world: when one is forced to ask the questions "why" and "how." These begin the process of learning and discovering answers that will help to recover the feeling of harmony with the world (Jarvis, 1987).

More recently, science has also tried to answer these questions, but the scientific answers are not altogether satisfying. We can investigate the cosmos through the technological marvels of modern telescopes—we can understand a little of its content and something of how the cosmos reached this stage in its creation, but it tells us nothing about the reason for its existence. We can study the human genome project and print out all six billion letters around our 25,000 genes, but what would it tell us about our humanity? With the proper training, it would tell us a lot about our physical bodies and our evolution, but nothing about our humanity or what it means to be human. Swartz (this volume) has begun to explore bridges between wisdom and science, but we will never be able to build that bridge completely, because science cannot provide empirical and demonstrable answers to these profound questions. Science seeks facts, but facts have no intrinsic meaning: we can give facts meaning and that is what the social construction of reality is all about.

We are faced with the problem that facts have no intrinsic meaning and yet both the cosmos and human existence are facts. Does this mean that our existence is meaningless? Is it just absurd? And is the cosmos meaningless—just some form of cosmological accident? Of course, there is no intrinsic meaning in the fact of our existence—in this sense, it is meaningless—and it matters not how much we know; we know that we will never understand the reasons for the cosmos or for humanity, if there are any. This is contrary to our commonsense view of the world. We might also ask whether the quest to discover meaning is itself absurd because we know that we will never discover that meaning. But this is also contrary to our inclination, which is to believe that this is not all absurd, meaningless, or accidental. It seems contrary to our reason, to our humanity, which seems to be on a perpetual quest to discover and answer the questions, "What's it all about?" and "How is it best to behave in this world?" Answers to these questions, then, are in the world of wisdom—the wise and the not so wise have tried to provide answers and guidance, and this we can study; indeed, it is what I used to teach. But I taught it from a Western viewpoint; answering these questions has been a universal quest, as Yang's chapter (this volume) shows. (See also Swartz, this volume, and Liu Wu-Chi, 1955).

New Directions for Adult and Continuing Education • DOI: 10.1002/ace

Despite not being able to provide answers to these questions, the knowledge society has placed its emphasis on scientific and technological knowledge and evidence-based practice. Lifelong learning has focused on those subjects seen to be useful in this present age, and religion and wisdom have been relegated to the periphery of educational concern. Recently, however, there has been a mini-revival of interest in the topic, which may also be regarded as a sign that we are moving beyond the reductive scientism of the knowledge society and that we can begin to appreciate that science and technology do not offer the only, or even an adequate, approach to the mysteries of both the cosmos and human beings. In the remainder of this chapter, therefore, I want to revisit some of the literature on wisdom that has been prevalent in the West: first from a religious/theological perspective (the "why") and second from a more practical perspective (the "how"); then I want to look at research, teaching, and learning. Finally, I want to return to this book itself.

Wisdom Literature: Seeking Answers

In Western societies, the wisdom literature most frequently referred to is that contained in Greek philosophy and in the Bible—especially the books of Ecclesiastes, Job, and Proverbs in the Old Testament, and the Wisdom of Solomon and the Wisdom of Ben Sira, both of which are in the apocrypha. However, any study of the Old Testament points us to an earlier wisdom, as reference is made, for instance, to "the wise men of Edom" (Obadiah, 8; Jeremiah, 49.v.7) and Anderson (1957, p. 465) makes the point that:

> The love of wisdom was not the monopoly of any one people of antiquity. The wisdom tradition is far more ancient than Socrates or anything found in the Old Testament. Furthermore the wisdom movement was essentially international. Wisdom writings circulated widely and had an influence far beyond the country of their origin.

Indeed, there are very close parallels between the Wisdom of Amen-em-ope, an Egyptian sage, and Proverbs 22.v.17 – 23.v.14 in the Bible (Anderson, 1957), indicating how Biblical writers utilized a wider literature for their own material. But not all wisdom is universal; it manifests itself in various cultures, as the wisdom of the Sisters of the Yam (Okpalaoka and Dillard, this volume) and Yang (this volume) each demonstrate. But we can see at least three major different types of wisdom in the Old Testament. There is the belief that the reasons for the universe are God's alone, for "the fear of Yahweh is the beginning of wisdom" (Proverbs 9.v.10) and "the beginning of knowledge" (Proverbs 1.v.7). This knowledge must lie with God, so the writers believed, and so these reasons cannot be discovered by mere mortals—God must reveal them. In a sociological sense, this is how the thinkers sought to legitimate their answers to these mysteries.

New Directions for Adult and Continuing Education • DOI: 10.1002/ace

But there is a second type of literature in the Old Testament that reflects the frustration that some thinkers experienced because they could not find answers to their questions: this resulted in a skeptical, questioning literature about the meaning of life and death. This is reflected in the book of Ecclesiastes, for instance, in which the frustrated author exclaimed that everything is vanity. But above all, this search is to be found in the book of Job, in which Job asked why he should live a good life in the face of considerable hardship and suffering. This also reflects the Babylonian and Egyptian traditions.

The third form of wisdom literature in the Old Testament is to be found in the often pithy one- and two-line sentences about aspects of human behavior and their outcomes, as in the book of Proverbs, or, in this volume, in Adam's story of Indra's net, in which everything in the world is an interconnected jewel (Daloz, this volume). Here we find wisdom about social living.

In Proverbs (1.vv.20ff), Wisdom appears in a different guise: a woman in the marketplace trying to spread her message to anybody who will listen; and so, through the ages, Wisdom has been personified in the form of a woman, as the title of Fraser and Hyland-Russell's chapter (this volume) implies. However, the author of Proverbs takes the analogy even further— for God founded the earth through wisdom. This is also reflected in the Prologue of John's gospel, in which the Word existed from the beginning. The personification of Wisdom has led to a sense that wisdom originates in the divine personage.

It is clear then that the ancient religions embodied the wisdom of the sages—and while we have concentrated here on the Western Judeo-Christian tradition rather than the Muslim tradition, there was certainly overlap in the medieval period. We might recall, for instance, that in A D 832, the Caliph of al-Ma'mun founded in Baghdad a House of Wisdom (MacIntyre, 2009, p. 44). But there is also a great tradition in the East, where we might look at Confucius (see Liu Wu-Chi, 1955, and Yang, this volume), amongst others. In India, we also need to look deeply at Hinduism and Buddhism, as Swartz (this volume) does to some extent.

More recently, Ford (2007) has argued that all Christian theology is wisdom, but since we suggested that wisdom is a profound human response to the mysteries of Being itself, we would claim that all religions and theologies are statements of wisdom. It is not only philosophers and theologians, however, who have been concerned about wisdom: wisdom has also traditionally been associated with the elders in society, and in more recent years, it has also become the province of psychologists and educators, amongst others.

The Wisdom of the Elders: Practical Wisdom

Life is a journey—a common metaphor—and the longer we travel on the way, the more we learn about it. Consequently, the learning of the elders has

New Directions for Adult and Continuing Education • DOI: 10.1002/ace

been regarded as a source of wisdom—practical wisdom, which is fundamentally different from the type of wisdom that seeks to answer the unanswerable questions about the mysteries of the cosmos. This is precisely the philosophy behind Aristotle's claim:

> What has been said is confirmed by the fact that while young men become geometricians and mathematicians and wise in matters like these, it is thought that a young man of practical wisdom cannot be found. The cause is that such wisdom is concerned not only with universals but with particulars, which become familiar from experience, but a young man has no experience, for it is length of time that gives experience . . . (Aristotle, 1925, VI.8, p.148).

However, it is not age *per se* that is the basis of practical wisdom but learning from experience; age is often related to experience, but it need not be because the circumstances of life provide the experiences from which we learn. We sometimes refer to young people as "wise beyond their years" and "having an old head on young shoulders," and to others of all ages as "streetwise." In these statements, we are referring to how individuals have learned from their experiences of life and, in a sense, these point to the possibility that all people can achieve wisdom within their cultural settings. Bassett (this volume) also refers to the wisdom of younger adults. Consequently, it is unwise to regard wisdom as a stage in the development of persons because of age or cognition.

Practical wisdom, however, is still regarded as the preserve of the elders in many countries in the world, especially those where traditional life styles are still valued. Thailand, for instance, has institutionalized the wisdom of the elders in its lifelong education system (Sungsri, 2009). It recognizes nine areas of traditional practical wisdom:

1. Agriculture
2. Industrial work and handicraft
3. Herbal doctors
4. Management of natural resources and environment
5. Community business and fundraising
6. Art and folk drama
7. Local language and literature
8. Philosophy, religions, and culture
9. Traditional Thai foods and sweets

All are taught freely in local wisdom centers, informally and non-formally, by recognized local providers of wisdom, who are usually people over fifty years of age. In Silpakorn University, and no doubt in other universities in Thailand, student teachers are also taught local wisdom. In Africa, wisdom is a preserve of the elders; there is a saying, "When an old person dies, a library burns down" (Hudson, 1999, p. 195). Wisdom is a mixture of knowledge and expertise learned as a result of everyday living and passed on from one generation to another through which seniors preserve traditional culture.

Vaillant (1993) discussed a similar role, the concept of "the keeper of meaning," which he regarded as "an objective indication of wisdom in older adults" (pp.158–160). He cited an example of Princeton Project 55, which was about mentoring. (See also Daloz, this volume.) Similarly, Parisi and others (2009) describe the Experience Corps, an intergenerational mentoring project designed to draw upon the wisdom of adults. Paradoxically, however, while mentoring has become a major function for experienced practitioners in the world of work, when companies downsize they tend to release the older members of their workforce, those who carry the subculture of the company within them and who often act as mentors to younger or less-experienced colleagues. Mentoring is a process of "using one's wisdom to support another" (Jarvis, 2001, p. 108) and the wise are experts in social living. But mentoring is also a process of using what we have learned to help us all live together and create a better world: wisdom entails morality.

Wisdom spans both religions and ethics; it is universal, finding its form and manifestation within specific cultures. It is not something for which we are hardwired through our evolution, but, as with other processes of learning, our acquisition of wisdom results in a process of soft-wiring in the brain, as Swartz's discussion (this volume) about neuroscience implies. It is associated with the aged but also with the experienced, and in this sense, practical wisdom underlies the mentoring process: it is intergenerational teaching and learning. In an aging society, we might learn to appreciate the wisdom of the elders once again, and this might lead to more research in this area. Perhaps also we will see educational gerontology courses becoming more integrated into traditional adult education, especially those courses devoted to the training of adult educators. However, in this rapidly changing Western world of science and technology, the wisdom of the elders lost a great deal of its status as older people became regarded as dispensable members of the workforce. Now Western society has to rediscover the humanity of the older people. We have to do this in a world that often moves too fast and does not give us sufficient time to contemplate or to engage with other people—or even with our own being. Only when we have the time can we learn spiritually engaged knowledge (Crawford, 2005), which might be regarded as wisdom. Sussman and Kossak (this volume) capture something of this in their discussion of the inner life and other chapters in this volume also focus on other aspects of spirituality.

Researching, Teaching, and Learning Wisdom

Wisdom, then, assumes at least two different forms—one explores the mystery of being, and the other provides a foundation for becoming. The former is philosophical/theological (*Sophia*) and the latter is ethical/cultural preservation (*phronesis*; see Tisdell, opening chapter, this volume.) *Phronesis* is also probably better understood as two distinct forms—cultivating intelligence in order to enhance the common good, and preserving successful cultural practices that maintain the unity and "wholeness" of the social group. It is difficult, therefore, to regard wisdom as a single, integrated whole except inasmuch as it is a response to the unknowns of existence itself. It is, therefore, difficult to research wisdom *per se*, although it is possible to research some of its characteristics in personality-type studies or even its socially recognized manifestations. However, biographical research projects may also prove a resource for wisdom studies. (See, for instance, the research of Alheit, 1995, and the "Learning from Our Lives" project in Scotland by Field, forthcoming).

But not all researchers of wisdom agree about its definition, as the authors in this volume demonstrate. Elsewhere, Ardelt (2000) sought to distinguish between intellectual and wisdom-related knowledge in six domains: goals, approach, range, acquisition, effects on the knower, and relation to age. She concluded that wisdom-related knowledge transcends time and is "practical knowledge of how to live a good life" (Ardelt, 2000, p. 785), whereas intellectual knowledge is often relative and changes in response to social conditions. But learning the ancient wisdom is an intellectual undertaking. Sternberg (2003, p. 152) also disagrees with Ardelt's distinction, since he regards wisdom as a form of successful intelligence:

> . . . the application of successful intelligence and creativity as mediated by values toward the achievement of the common good through a balance among (a) intrapersonal, (b) interpersonal, and (c) extra-personal interests, over (a) short and (b) long terms, in order to achieve a balance among (a) adaptation to existing environments, (b) shaping of existing environments, and (c) selection of new environments . . .

Sternberg (2003) is concerned with practical wisdom, which he suggests is "successful intelligence balancing goals, responses, and interests . . . in order to seek the common good" (p. 153). This is his "balancing theory," but, significantly, he omits age and experience from his understanding of the phenomenon unless they are included within his concept of "successful intelligence." However, he also includes both in his understanding of how/when that knowledge and creativity should be employed. The place of intelligence in relation to wisdom is by no means self-evident, as we have already pointed out with reference to such expressions as "streetwise." In addition, it should be recognized that "the common good" is not an objective phenomenon but a subjective assessment of the ends of being or of the immediate ends of specific social behavior. Parisi and others (2009), in contrast, also suggest that wisdom is a combination of individual, experiential, and facilitative factors that result in successful aging, but in this instance "successful" refers to teaching successful "good" actions across the generations. In almost all discussions on practical wisdom, the common good plays a significant role, even though this is a contentious concept—the "how" of practical wisdom is nearly always grounded in social ethics rather than intelligence, and it is usually learned from experience.

A number of authors, such as Sternberg (2003) and some authors in this volume (see Bassett, and Fraser and Hyland-Russell), suggest that wisdom can be taught in schools and colleges. Certainly the theological, philosophical, and ethical answers to the questions of being and becoming can be taught as academic rather than faith-related subjects, either separately or as part of curriculum of other subjects, as Sternberg suggests. While we can teach both about the manifestations and the characteristics of wisdom in schools, we have to recognize that this approach to formal education will only allow learners to have knowledge of wisdom rather than to be wise. In experiential education, however, learners have the opportunity of growing in wisdom, and this is part of the reason why I have always emphasized experiential learning in my own work. I could teach wisdom in knowledge-based subjects, and the students might acquire knowledge of wisdom, but through experiential learning they can also grow and develop as persons (Jarvis, 2009)—perhaps becoming a little more wise in the process. Experiential learning allows for the growth in practical wisdom. This is true of all learners, but educators need to be trained to help learners reflect upon their experiences. There is, therefore, space in the educational process for learners to grow in wisdom, but it is space best created by experienced teachers (see Fraser and Hyland-Russell, this volume).

Much wisdom, however, is not learned intentionally—it is acquired as an element in our learning from our own lives, often incidentally and even almost unconsciously, in the process of daily living. In this sense, it is tacit. Daily living is actually a very complex process of experiencing action and interaction, conforming to norms and mores and deciding when to break them and do something different, and so on. It is a process whereby we build up a repertoire of forms of behavior we know to be useful, but it is also one in which we remember unconsciously many other useful aspects of our everyday experiences; in this, we build up a store of tacit knowledge that expands with age and experience. This tacit repertoire forms an integral part of the wisdom of the experienced, even aged; this knowledge is learned but not always learned through teaching. There is a profound difference between knowing about wisdom and being wise—for being wise is an ontological condition, but those who achieve it may not always be aware of the nature of their achievement, although others may recognize it.

Conclusion

The chapters in this volume have presented many different facets of wisdom—they do not always agree with each other, but they demonstrate the diverse ways in which it may be studied. Wisdom seeks to provide answers to these fundamental existential questions, but so too does philosophy—the love of wisdom. Philosophers engage in extensive debates about the truth of their claims, and perhaps this book—important in its own right in adding to the small volume of studies on the subject—will also point the way to more philosophical studies in the field of adult education.

References

Alheit, P. "Biographical Learning: Theoretical Outline, Challenges and Contradictions of a New Approach to Adult Education." In P. Alheit, A. Bron-Wojciechowska, E. Brugger, and P. Dominice (eds.), *The Biographical Approach in European Adult Education*. Vienna: Verband Wiener Volksbildung, 1995.

Anderson, B. *The Living World of the Old Testament*. Englewood Cliffs, N.J.: Prentice Hall, 1957.

Ardelt, M. "Intellectual versus Wisdom-Related Knowledge: The Case for a Different Kind of Learning in the Later Years of Life." *Educational Gerontology*, 2000, 26(8), 771–789.

Aristotle. *The Nicemedian Ethics*. Oxford, U.K.: Oxford University Press, 1925.

Crawford, J. *Spiritually Engaged Knowledge*. Ashgate. U.K.: Aldershot, 2005.

Field, J. "Learning from Our Lives." In P. Jarvis and M. Watts (eds.), *The Routledge International Handbook of Learning*. London: Routledge, forthcoming.

Ford, D. *Christian Wisdom*. Cambridge, U.K.: Cambridge University Press, 2007.

Hudson, F. *The Adult Years*. San Francisco: Jossey Bass, 1999.

Jarvis, P. *Learning in the Social Context*. London: Croom Helm, 1987.

Jarvis, P. *Learning in Later Life*. London: Kogan Page, 2001.

Jarvis, P. *Learning to Be a Person in Society*. London: Routledge, 2009.

Liu, W-C. *A Short History of Confucian Philosophy*. Harmondsworth, U.K.: Penguin, 1955.

MacIntyre, A. *God, Philosophy, Universities*. London: Continuum, 2009.

Parisi, J., Rebok, G., Carlson, M., Fried, L., Seeman, T., Tan, E., Tenner, E., and Piferi, R. "Can the Wisdom of Aging Be Activated and Make a Difference Societally?" *Educational Gerontology*, 2009, 35(10), 867–879.

Pasternak, C. "Curiosity and Quest." In C. Pasternak (ed.), *What Makes Us Human?* Oxford, U.K.: One World, 2007.

Polanyi, M. *The Tacit Dimension*. London: Routledge and Kegan Paul, 1967.

Sternberg, R. *Wisdom, Intelligence, and Creativity Synthesized*. Cambridge, U.K.: Cambridge University Press, 2003.

Sungsri, S. "The Role of Local Wisdom in Promoting Lifelong Learning in Thailand." ASEM Lifelong Learning Network 4 Conference Presentation, Riga, Latvia, 2009.

Vaillant, G. *The Wisdom of the Ego*. Cambridge, Mass.: Harvard University Press, 1993.

PETER JARVIS *is emeritus professor of continuing education, University of Surrey, U.K.*

INDEX

Page references followed by *fig* indicate an illustrated figure.

accommodate the needs of adult students. These programs combine academic rigor with applied knowledge, scholarship, convenience, and flexibility and come in a variety of formats. The colleges and universities—public and private, nonprofit and for-profit—that respond to this increasing market have discovered both a surprising number of committed students and a new revenue stream. This volume of *New Directions for Adult and Continuing Education* explores the emergence of the nontraditional doctoral degree, the characteristics of the nontraditional doctoral student, faculty concerns, program innovation, and unique programs at four institutions. Both scholars and practitioners will find it an interesting and engaging introduction to the topic.
ISBN: 978-1-1180-2763-9

ACE128   **The Struggle for Democracy in Adult Education**
Dianne Ramdeholl, Tania Giordani, Thomas Heaney, Wendy Yanow
Adult education in the United States has its roots in democracy. Early in the twentieth century, adult education was often described as a "movement," a spontaneous emergence of study circles, town hall meetings, and learning groups, all engaged in better understanding their world to build a better one democratically. Education in its broadest sense—learning to name the world—was at the center of that movement.
   At the same time, and at the opposite end of the spectrum, were those who made the leap from lifelong learning to lifelong schooling. Collapse of the almost-movement was inevitable. Educators in the workplace and in formal institutions of learning sought to shape minds, rather than free them. Consequently, adult education grew up alongside a practice that devalued learning for democratic action and stressed adaptation to the workplace, corporate America, and a consumer economy.
   Perhaps nostalgia is a lingering desire to return to a past that never was, but many adult educators, including the authors represented in this volume, have been attempting to reclaim their birthright—a critical but steadfast commitment to building democracy. In this book we build on the historic relationship between adult education and democracy. We examine an adult education practice that not only shapes minds, but also seeks to build communities of collaborative action. We explore best practices in shared and informed decision making within different contexts of adult education—in the community, the classroom, and the university—by focusing on various aspects of our work as adult education practitioners.
ISBN: 978-1-1180-0302-2

ACE127   **Adult Education in Cultural Institutions: Aquariums, Libraries, Museums, Parks, and Zoos**
Edward W. Taylor, Marilyn McKinley Parrish
On any given week millions of adults around the world can be found gathering in libraries, parks, zoos, arboretums, and museums in person or online. These cultural institutions are seen as repositories of knowledge and collections of a community's cultural or natural heritage. However, they are much more. They are structures that promote cognitive change: commons, places of community outside of home and work, where individuals and groups gather to share and discuss ideas. Cultural institutions may be sites of conflict and contestation where economic and political challenges call into question institutional purpose and mission, and debates emerge over whose story is told.

They can also serve as sites of deliberative democracy that foster social change and reform, where community members can engage with challenging and important societal issues. This volume aims to forge a stronger relationship between adult educators and educators within cultural institutions in an effort to better understand adult learning and teaching within these sites of nonformal education and the role these institutions play in society.
ISBN: 978-0-4709-5208-5

ACE126 Narrative Perspectives on Adult Education

Marsha Rossiter, M. Carolyn Clark

This volume presents a variety of perspectives on the role of narrative in adult learning and explores how those perspectives can be translated into practice. Interest in narrative among adult educators has been a continuing strand of our professional dialogue for some time, and it continues to grow as we become increasingly appreciative of the multifaceted views of adult learning that are revealed through the narrative lens. The range of narrative applications, implications, and perspectives in adult education is practically limitless. The perspectives included in this sourcebook, while not an exhaustive review, do convey something of the rich variety and scope a narrative approach offers adult learning.
ISBN: 978-0-4708-7465-3

ACE125 White Privilege and Racism: Perceptions and Actions

Carole L. Lund, Scipio A. J. Colin, III

White privilege is viewed by many as a birthright and is in essence an existentialist norm that is based upon the power and privilege of pigmentation. Because it is the norm for the white race, this privilege is virtually invisible, but its racist byproducts are not. It becomes common for whites to believe falsely that their privilege was earned by hard work and intellectual superiority; it becomes the center of their worldview. The reality is that when they defend their pigmentary privilege, what they are really saying is that peoples of color have earned their disadvantage. Unless whites recognize this privilege and the consequent racist attitudes and behaviors, they will continue to perpetuate racism in both their personal and professional lives. It is their responsibility to commit to a significant paradigm shift by recognizing their privilege, critiquing the impact on peoples of color, and making the decision to reconfigure their attitudes and alter their behaviors. This volume focuses on facilitating our understanding of the conceptual correlation between white privilege and racism and how these intertwined threads are manifested in selected areas of adult and continuing education practice. Although there seems to be a consensus that this practice reflects sociocultural and intellectual racism, there has been no discussion of linkages between the white racist ideology, white privilege, and white attitudes and behaviors behind that racism.
ISBN: 978-0-4706-3162-1

ACE124 Reaching Out Across the Border: Canadian Perspectives in Adult Education

Patricia Cranton, Leona M. English

This volume brings together Canadian scholars and practitioners to articulate a variety of historical, geographical, and political positions on the field of adult education in Canada. The chapter authors examine the country's interests and discourses and detail Canada's history,

educational initiatives, movements, and linguistic struggles. Specifically, the authors address the uniqueness of Canada's emphasis on linking health and adult literacy; the use of video and dialogue to promote adult and literacy education in the North; the historical adult education initiatives such as Frontier College and the Antigonish movement; the special language and cultural issues that define Quebec's role of adult education and training; the development of critical adult education discourse in Canada; the emphasis on environmental adult education; the uniqueness of the community college system; and initiatives in adult education for community development. By describing Canadian accomplishments and lessons learned in adult education, this volume will help inform the practice, research, and studies of adult educators in the United States.
ISBN: 978-0-4705-9259-5

ACE123   Negotiating Ethical Practice in Adult Education

Elizabeth J. Burge
Here is a collection for twenty-first-century challenges! One practical philosopher and seven experienced adult educators dig into their driving values, the existing literature, and frank narratives of direct experience to illuminate key lessons in being one's own applied ethicist. In explaining their decision-making and confronting their unease and doubts, the authors emerge as self-aware, context-aware, principled practitioners. But they are not immune to the problems encountered in the intellectual and interpersonal complexities of ethical analysis.

Acknowledging the challenges in moving beyond such reductionist analyses as "right versus wrong," the authors look for negotiated possibilities of "rightness." Negotiation, reflection, and power emerge as three key themes of the reflective chapters. As a reader, you might consider the various thinking strategies offered, in particular the strategy of "sinning bravely." Additional critical thinking about conflicts that hide in the background of our work ought to help unearth some hegemonic uses of concepts such as fairness and justice.

Feel encouraged, feel strong, feel connected as you compare your own issues and thinking with the authors' experience and guidance. The reading journey of this issue of *New Directions for Adult and Continuing Education* will bring you closer to possibilities for more good work in the tough conditions of twenty-first-century adult education.
ISBN: 978-0-4705-3971-2

ACE122   Social Capital and Women's Support Systems: Networking, Learning, and Surviving

Carmela R. Nanton, Mary V. Alfred
The concept of social capital goes back to the early twentieth century. Although it has sociological underpinnings, it has been primarily applied in the business arena. Increasingly, over the last two decades, there has been a proliferation of literature that proposes a broader application of the social capital concepts to individuals, communities, societies, and even adult learning.

This monograph applies social capital concepts to women as adult learners in learning communities, as users of technology, and as workers, and then integrates it from the perspective of adult education. We make the case that, because women tend to be more relational than men, their lives as students are integrally related to the social networks of which they are a part. We recognize that there are certain risks inherent in social capital networks and that gender bias can lead

to exclusionary challenges that marginalize women as a group. On that basis, some feminist theorists have suggested that we simply eliminate the idea of social capital because of the inherent bias in the theory's underlying concepts and assumptions. Instead, we propose an integrationist approach that recognizes the relational nature of women, their historical and contemporary use of social capital networks, and the way they leverage such relationships for personal and community transformation.
ISBN: 978-0-4705-3734-3

ACE 121 Bringing Community to the Adult ESL Classroom
Clarena Larrotta, Ann K. Brooks
Using the concept of community building as a framework, this volume summarizes and updates readers on the state of adult English as a second language (ESL) education in the United States. It provides a complete description of this population of learners and their learning needs. The various chapters discuss possibilities for community building in the adult ESL classroom, combining research, theory, and practice. Community building is not a new topic; we often discuss it informally with our colleagues and students. However, scant written material exists—with a focus on adult ESL—documenting how it happens or reconciling theory with practitioners' experiences. In this volume, several practitioners and researchers explain the ways in which they use community-building principles in adult ESL settings. The authors' descriptions of applications of community-building principles can help other adult educators implement these ideas in their teaching practice. Our goal is to encourage readers to spark conversation and continuous learning among all who work in this field.
ISBN: 978-0-4704-7955-1

ACE120 Adult Learning and the Emotional Self
John M. Dirkx
Emotion is a pervasive force in adult learning—from fear, anxiety, dread, shame, and doubt to hope, excitement, joy, desire, and pride. For the most part, however, practitioners and scholars view the adult learning process as conceptual, rational, and cognitive. If emotion is considered positively, it is as a helpful adjunct to the learning process. More often, it is regarded as a potential barrier that has to be worked through if effective learning is to occur. Although we are only beginning to attend to the powerful role that emotion can play in our lives as teachers and adult learners, a small but growing body of interdisciplinary scholarship provides an opportunity to revisit our earlier assumptions. This volume seeks to build on this emerging scholarship by focusing on the emotional self across a range of adult learning settings: basic and higher education, workplace learning, and formal and informal contexts. The chapters demonstrate, in different ways, the growing integration of emotion into more holistic, constructive ways of learning and knowing. As we attune to the emotional atmosphere in which we work, we stand a better chance of helping adult students achieve their educational goals—and we become better educators in the process.
ISBN: 978-0-4704-4674-4

NEW DIRECTIONS FOR ADULT AND CONTINUING EDUCATION

ORDER FORM SUBSCRIPTION AND SINGLE ISSUES

DISCOUNTED BACK ISSUES:

Use this form to receive 20% off all back issues of *New Directions for Adult and Continuing Education*.
All single issues priced at **$23.20** (normally $29.00)

TITLE   ISSUE NO.   ISBN

_____   _____   _____

_____   _____   _____

_____   _____   _____

*Call 888-378-2537 or see mailing instructions below. When calling, mention the promotional code JBNND
to receive your discount. For a complete list of issues, please visit www.josseybass.com/go/ndace*

SUBSCRIPTIONS: (1 YEAR, 4 ISSUES)

☐ New Order   ☐ Renewal

U.S.	☐ Individual: $89	☐ Institutional: $259
CANADA/MEXICO	☐ Individual: $89	☐ Institutional: $299
ALL OTHERS	☐ Individual: $113	☐ Institutional: $333

*Call 888-378-2537 or see mailing and pricing instructions below.
Online subscriptions are available at www.onlinelibrary.wiley.com*

ORDER TOTALS:

Issue / Subscription Amount: $ _____

Shipping Amount: $ _____
(for single issues only – subscription prices include shipping)

Total Amount: $ _____

SHIPPING CHARGES:	
First Item	$5.00
Each Add'l Item	$3.00

*(No sales tax for U.S. subscriptions. Canadian residents, add GST for subscription orders. Individual rate subscriptions must
be paid by personal check or credit card. Individual rate subscriptions may not be resold as library copies.)*

BILLING & SHIPPING INFORMATION:

☐ **PAYMENT ENCLOSED:** *(U.S. check or money order only. All payments must be in U.S. dollars.)*

☐ **CREDIT CARD:**   ☐ VISA   ☐ MC   ☐ AMEX

Card number _____Exp. Date_____

Card Holder Name_____Card Issue # _____

Signature _____Day Phone _____

☐ **BILL ME:** *(U.S. institutional orders only. Purchase order required.)*

Purchase order # _____
Federal Tax ID 13559302 • GST 89102-8052

Name_____

Address_____

Phone_____ E-mail_____

Copy or detach page and send to: **John Wiley & Sons, PTSC, 5th Floor**
989 Market Street, San Francisco, CA 94103-1741

Order Form can also be faxed to: **888-481-2665**

PROMO JBNND